# A LONG LETTING GO

MARILYN CHANDLER MCENTYRE

# A LONG
# LETTING GO

*Meditations on Losing Someone You Love*

WILLIAM B. EERDMANS PUBLISHING COMPANY

GRAND RAPIDS, MICHIGAN / CAMBRIDGE, U.K.

Published 2015 by
Wm. B. Eerdmans Publishing Co.
2140 Oak Industrial Drive N.E., Grand Rapids, Michigan 49505 /
P.O. Box 163, Cambridge CB3 9PU U.K.

Printed in the United States of America

21  20  19  18  17  16  15      7  6  5  4  3  2  1

**Library of Congress Cataloging-in-Publication Data**

McEntyre, Marilyn Chandler, 1949-
A long letting go: meditations on losing someone you love /
Marilyn Chandler McEntyre.
pages        cm
ISBN 978-0-8028-7310-1 (pbk.: alk. paper)
1. Caregivers — Religious life — Meditations.  2. Loss (Psychology) —
Religious aspects — Christianity — Meditations.  3. Death — Religious aspects —
Christianity — Meditations.  4. Bereavement — Meditations.    I. Title.

BV4910.9.M34  2015
242'.4 — dc23

2015009845

www.eerdmans.com

*In memory of my mother, Mary,*

*who taught me to care by caring, with generosity and grace,*

*for the many she watched through their final days.*

~

*And for John,*

*who has walked the hard last mile with others,*

*and may, someday, with me.*

~

*And for our children — including the one who is gone —*

*whose lives shape and enrich our own.*

# CONTENTS

# *The Care We're Called To*

At some point in our lives, most of us will become caregivers. It is a vocation that can last for a few weeks of recovery time or for a long period of chronic illness or disability, and it will involve us intimately in another's preparation for death. For us, too, it is preparation for a letting go that draws upon our deepest spiritual resources in ways impossible to fully anticipate.

This gathering of reflections for caregivers focuses on the season of death and the strenuous, challenging, life-changing work of accompanying a beloved friend or family member on the final stretch of his or her journey and of mourning the losses that come at every stage. The reflections are rooted in my own experience of caring for family members who have died, keeping deathwatch with friends in times of loss, and serving as a hospice volunteer — humbling work that leaves me, after every visit and vigil, feeling privileged to be permitted into others' sacred time and space.

These pieces are written primarily for those who believe in Christ and his promises, but they may also serve others — who come from other faith communities or from none — who happen upon them when life presents them with the task of caregiving. They are meant not as advice, nor as theological statement, but simply as a harvest of experiences and reflections that may provide some direction, hope, or consolation in a time when generosity, imagination, patience, and love may be stretched in unprecedented ways.

The first section, "Accompanying," focuses on various ways in which both the person who is dying and the person called to be present during that process may find themselves challenged, surprised, and invited into new understandings of faith and faithfulness.

The second section, "Stories of Letting Go," offers a handful of short stories from the bedside that illumine moments of learning how to let go and how to receive the grace that is given in just such times.

The third section, "Mourning," focuses on the work of mourning, which, like caregiving, may be more complex, surprising, and paradoxically life-giving than one imagines beforehand.

The fourth section, "Words for Keeping Watch," offers prayers that might serve not only to articulate longings and needs that arise as one keeps watch but also as grounding points for the diffuse feelings and thoughts that arise in the course of a long letting go.

May you who are called in these moments of your life to confer a final blessing find some blessing here.

# ACCOMPANYING

# Setting the House in Order

*In those days Hezekiah became sick and was at the point of death. And Isaiah the prophet the son of Amoz came to him and said to him, "Thus says the LORD, 'Set your house in order, for you shall die; you shall not recover.'"*

2 KINGS 20:1

Isaiah's task wasn't easy. Delivering bad news never is. For one thing, it's not always clear when to do so. Though doctors are more likely now than a few decades ago to deliver terminal prognoses frankly, family members and friends still have the delicate task of discerning when and how to help a beloved one come to terms with death. Especially when there is significant unfinished business, knowing that recovery is highly unlikely allows for re-orientation, reconciliation, and practical and spiritual preparation. But, especially now, when medical interventions can continue long beyond the borders of reasonable hope, denial can persist beyond where it is useful, and foreclose the precious conversations with self and others that often happen in the final days.

Denial is a powerful and sometimes necessary psychological tool. Sometimes hard truths need to be postponed. Medical ethics boards have had many an argument about when and whether to deliver the stark message that Isaiah delivers to Hezekiah. As it happens, Hezekiah did recover, but the prophet's words served a purpose beyond what he evidently recognized. "You shall die" is a hard pronouncement, but it can be a liberating one if it can be offered and understood as a calling.

Even dying is a calling. For some it is a time to give and receive forgiveness. For some it is a time to recall and claim the reassurances that faith provides. For some it is a time to see visions and dream dreams. Some need companionship; some, solitude. Some sleep, some remain wakeful, and some toss, restless and uneasy, between the two, enduring their going hence as infants endure the discomfort of the birth canal.

The companionship we can offer — those of us who keep vigil — needs to begin with discernment, a humble seeking of the call of the moment. Is this a time to speak, or a time to open and guard a spacious silence? Is it a time to invoke God's protection, Jesus' consolation, and the Spirit's guidance, or a time to tell stories that reaffirm the goodness of this life, now ending, so that the person dying may leave it with gratitude? Is it a time to share the burden of sorrow, or a time to postpone lament to protect serenity? Is it a time to come, like Isaiah, with a clear, practical, challenging word of truth, or a time to allow for the weakness we share as humans who, as T. S. Eliot said, "cannot bear very much reality"?

Discernment is prayerful work: *Help me notice what is needed. Help me to lay aside my own besetting anguish and be available for that need. Help me recognize that another's need may be very different from my own. Help me, as I watch, to stay awake to the changes that come about in this mysterious process and respond to them generously, patiently, and selflessly. Help me open my own heart to receive the grace I need to respond to the demands of this day. Help me to recognize both the work of dying and the work of watching as honorable and sacred tasks.*

Hospice volunteers who keep vigil at the bedsides of dying patients are warned when they are trained that they may be asked to leave before the final hour, to allow the family privacy for the last good-byes. However connected they may feel to the person dying, they may not have the closure of witnessing the final breath or speaking the final word of reassurance. And sometimes no one gets that closure. Many who are dying seem to wait until all witnesses — even the most dearly loved — are out of the room to release their final breath. Dying has its own kinds of diplomacy.

Denise Levertov's phrase "patient, courteously waiting Death" introduces the unusual idea that there are courtesies to be recognized and practiced in the hour of death. And courtesy is rooted in kindness, and kindness in discernment, and discernment in prayer. Small courtesies — offering ice chips, straightening sheets, lowering lights and voices — may be done with great love. We never know how large or small our gifts and offerings really are. We don't need to. Our work is to accept and attend the call of each moment and allow these moments, like all others, to arrive and depart in God's good time.

*You who came in divine humility,*
*give me the humility now*
*to relinquish all vain efforts to control this going,*
*to remain watchful without agitation,*
*to remain attentive without anxiety,*
*to be a companion on this final journey*
*and take my leave when it is time*
*with hope and grace. Amen.*

## Facing Fear

*My heart is in anguish within me;*
*the terrors of death have fallen upon me.*

PSALM 55:4

The gentle, demanding work of caring for the dying often includes coming to terms with both their fear and your own. Some of the most faithful, prayerful Christians I know are afraid of death. One survey revealed that among Americans, fear of death is second only to fear of public speaking — a fact I find both puzzling and amusing. It may also seem puzzling that those who have put their trust in the Lord, and who believe Christ came to call us into a covenant of immeasurable grace, and that he went to prepare a place for us, still dread leaving this life for the next. My ninety-four-year-old grandmother, a devout Baptist and Bible reader all her life, tired and debilitated in her great age, went gently but certainly not eagerly into "that good night." There aren't many who can say, as Thomas More did to his executioner when asked how he could be so sure he was going to God, "He will not refuse one who is so blithe to go to him."

But fear of death has little to do with a lack of faith. Like fear of a steep cliff or deep water or a dark wood, fear of death has to do with not knowing what lies beyond. It is deeply natural to cling to the known, cherished goodness of this life over against the unknown, very like the way a child clings to its mother's skirts for a while before risking a solitary venture into the wider world. In the absence of palpable evidence to the contrary, it is hard not to imagine death as loss: loss of control, loss of those we love, loss of the particular pleasures that have made life worth living, loss of opportunities, loss of the future we imagined.

Scripture, in addition to acknowledging the "terrors," also offers specific assurances. "Neither life nor death . . . nor any other thing can separate us from the love of God that is in Christ Jesus." "Though I walk in the valley of the shadow of death, I will fear no evil, for Thou art with me." "Love is strong as death." "For if we have been united with him in a death like his, we shall certainly be united with him in a resurrection like his." These assurances are worth claiming when it is our loved one's turn to walk that valley.

There are other kinds of reassurance. Over the years I've been privileged to hear several stories of after-death contact told by credible and thoughtful people. One such story came from a sensible and pious German friend of mine. She told me about her friend of many years who appeared minutes after a fatal car accident to say *"Ich bin gut angekommen"* ("I have arrived safely"). I have also found solace in stories of "near-death experiences," of which there are many. Most of these accounts by people who "died" on operating tables or in accidents and came back are remarkably reassuring. Most of these individuals reported that they found themselves in a state of deep peace; that they were drawn toward a light; that they were accompanied by a kindly and loving presence, sometimes appearing as someone they knew, other times not; that they were welcomed; that they felt completely loved; that when they returned, it was with some reluctance, but also with a sense of purpose; that that sense of purpose remained when they awoke again in this world; and that they have never since been afraid of death. Though not universal, and not scientifically verifiable, there are too many of these stories to ignore. And though they are not uniform, they do remind us that, as George Herbert wrote, "Love bids us welcome."

A Holocaust survivor I had the privilege of knowing once told me, "When you have come face to face with your own death and accepted it, you are free." She was speaking psychologically. To speak theologically adds a dimension to that important affirmation: death is a passage to new life. No vision or version of life in that next dimension is likely to convey the whole truth. It remains as mysterious as Jesus' assurances that heaven is "near" and "within you" and "among you" and a "place" where we are awaited. But while we who remain to live a little longer peer through a glass darkly, we may see enough to assure us that the life that awaits us all is richer and more real than anything we know.

*Loving God, _____ is your child.*
*Calm her fear of the dark.*
*Be present to her as she drifts into sleep.*

*Stay with her through the night.*
*We commit her to your care, and all those she loves and*
       *fears losing,*
*all the work she has not finished,*
*all the days that remain to her,*
*including the last.*
*You who died for us and before us,*
*meet her when she dies, we pray,*
*and welcome her home. Amen.*

# The Long Letting Go

*And about the time of her death the women attending*
*her said to her, "Do not be afraid, for you have borne a*
*son." But she did not answer or pay attention.*

1 SAMUEL 4:20

As I sat with my father one day not long before he died, realizing he seemed to be fully aware, but unaware of me or of anyone else passing through the room, this startling thought came to me: *He doesn't need us anymore.* He was strongly focused on something, it seemed, but not on us. Like Phinehas's wife in the Samuel story, who does not answer or pay attention, he had in some way already left us.

There remained many moments of connection, affection, and preparation before he died, but the sense that his face was already set "toward Jerusalem" and that we were receding into his peripheral vision remained. Of course there were needs. He needed to be resituated in bed, he needed a little water now and then, he needed to hear my mother's voice, and I like to think he needed and wanted to hear the Psalms we read as he lay half-asleep. But already he was beyond our human help. To say that is to recall not despair, but the simple clarity of that moment when the common assurance "He is in God's hands" struck me as simply, utterly, observably true.

There is great pathos in the story of Phinehas's wife, who dies in fresh grief over the loss of her father-in-law and husband even as she endures the pains of childbirth. Part of that pathos lies in the futile efforts of the midwives to revive her into rejoicing over her newborn son. Even the greatest human joys and sorrows recede into irrelevancy, as they must, as the dying are guided toward a different light and a different life.

Toward the very end of my mother's long life, I found her decreasing interest in grandchildren and great-grandchildren painful at first, and then instructive. She had a spacious, loving heart for all of us. She had taken due and natural delight in our babies and their babies, holding and rocking and reading and laughing as grandmothers do, making special pancakes for their visits and keeping a costume box in the closet for the pleasure of little girls. But as death approached, her inquiries about those beloved granddaughters and their families became perfunctory, and her attention wandered as I eagerly reported that Stephen was learning to ride a bike, that Matthew had said a new sentence, that Tommy's parents were playing him Mozart — all the sweet, small bits of news she had once reveled in.

But she had work to do that required all that was left of her earthly energies. Her quiet preoccupation reminded me of Jesus' words to his mother, who finds him in the temple after seeking him frantically for three days: "Know you not that I must be about my father's business?" The question challenges her, and us, to recognize the contingent character of even the most intimate human relationships: *My work here isn't, finally, about you. I'm here on a mission, as you are, that requires and deserves my full attention.*

It's natural for us to try to re-engage our dying family folk in the life they're leaving by reminding them of memories and showing them pictures, assuming they want to reminisce — and many do, up to a point. But when that point is past, tugging at them may be a distraction from the arduous, demanding, and perhaps — who knows? — exhilarating business of turning inward and heavenward, listening hard for the comforts and summonings that come from elsewhere, and leaving us behind.

The instruction I received from my mother's curious indifference was simple: *Let her go where she needs to go.* Much of her story had to do with us. This part of it didn't. Day after day she prayed for us when we lived far away, releasing us into lives that for long stretches had little to do with her. Now it was our turn to do the same, across the increasing distance between us, releasing her to those who awaited her and renewing our own consent to the work that remained for us here.

*May we let go when the time comes.*
*May we wait in trust as long as parting takes.*
*May we be present without demands.*
*May we put all we love in God's hands.*
*May we let ourselves be blessed even in loss.*
*May we be open to peace*

*that passes all understanding*
*and eases our anguish*
*and keeps our hearts open. Amen.*

# A Generous Dying

*By faith Jacob, when dying, blessed each of the sons of Joseph. . . .*

HEBREWS 11:21

Generosity seems an odd word to apply to the process of dying, and perhaps an inappropriate expectation of those whose time has come to die. Still, I have been moved at several bedsides by the way those who were dying extended generosity to those already grieving their loss. They extended comfort, as if from a place of privilege, to those they were leaving behind. They had come to their own peace with death; they were moving into a new life; they had "turned their faces toward Jerusalem," and were on their way. We who remained were the ones seeking solace, and they offered it. From a place beyond physical pain, expending dwindling energy, they stretched out willing hands to be held, spoke words of love and consolation, and allowed our tears.

We speak of caring for the dying, and many of us do, or have, or will. It is an honor to provide that kind of care, and it can also be arduous work, especially in a time of prolonged illness and suffering. But it seems to me that we speak less, and perhaps not enough, of the ways the dying care for us who, for a time, remain. The kinds of generous care for the living I have received and witnessed include these:

*Willingness to witness our grief.* I remember vividly the look of kindness and pity (in the full, ancient, spacious sense of that word) a dying friend gave both her husband and me as we watched over her together for a time. She held our hands and watched our tears fall. Though wide awake and responsive to us and to our sorrow, she seemed untroubled. She had, in the previous weeks, and after her own struggle over losing all she loved in this life, shifted her efforts from staying alive to letting go. She was further along that path than we, and became in that hour our teacher and guide through the hard places of loss. There was a quiet generosity in her consent to be with us in our sorrow, especially since she had borne so much of her own. That particular kindness has become part of her legacy to me.

*Tact.* Dying, like any other life event, is a social situation to be negotiated between people whose needs and sensitivities differ. I was impressed with what I could only think of as exceptional tact on the part of a hospice patient I was visiting one day when another visitor appeared with what struck me (rather uncharitably) as forced cheerfulness: too much chatter, and a nervous, fussy need to do something that stirred the air around us as she plumped pillows, rearranged flowers, and adjusted the window blinds. He bore with all this kindly, answered her questions, and offered her, it seemed, something of his own deep calm. He didn't once object, though he was visibly fatigued. A certain courtliness, rooted perhaps in awareness of her own suffering, enabled him to accept her efforts and her intentions without objection, though they added little to his own physical comfort. I remembered the funny, honest words of a Quaker woman who rose once in a meeting and said, "I want to say a good word for muddling through. It's what we do." I thought about how we muddle through the occasions that take us to the edge of our emotional comfort zones and the social conventions that put us at ease. Dying takes us into deep places of the heart and spirit, and it's good to go there. But the smaller matters of where to sit, how long to stay, and what to say require a tact on both sides that deserves to be recognized as one of the many forms of life-giving love we continue to need.

*Honesty.* Tact at its best is informed by honesty. One of the gifts of a gradual going is the opportunity it may afford for conversations that have been postponed or truths that have been suppressed out of fear or family custom or the inertia of habit. The honesty of the dying is a gift to the living — even, sometimes, when it is painful. A grandmother may ask to see one grandchild rather than another for reasons she may not always share. I remember also hearing of the surprising forthrightness of a young mother who, knowing the practicalities of death, reminded her husband about what happens after death, what kind of equipment and attention might be required before hospice nurses or the coroner came, and what the children might need to be protected from seeing. Her clarity, though it stung in the moment, was an offering he found helpful when the time came, and he looked back on her unabashed foresight as one of her many acts of courage.

In a final, unevenly scrawled note to me days before her death, a beloved mentor left me with advice I continue to recall with gratitude: "Live boldly. Live generously." As I have witnessed more dying, I have come to recognize how those admonitions may serve as guides for living even the final days. Dying can be bold and generous. When it is, the loss it brings can be laced with gratitude.

*Gracious God, I thank you for the ways that _____ has blessed me, taking leave with such kindness. Help me to learn from this generous dying how to live generously, even in the days of my own grieving. Amen.*

# A Good Death

*"Let me die the death of the upright, and let my end be like his!"*

NUMBERS 23:10

Both Catholic and Protestant prayer books have traditionally included prayers for a good death. One Catholic prayer includes petitions for "perfect sorrow, sincere contrition, remission of our sins, a worthy reception of the most holy Viaticum, the strengthening of the Sacrament of Extreme Unction, so that we may be able to stand with safety before the throne of the just but merciful Judge, our God and our Redeemer." A similar prayer used in the Anglican tradition includes petitions for "a full discharge from all his sins, who most earnestly begs it of Thee," and removal of "whatever is corrupt in him through human frailty, or by the snares of the enemy."

These prayers emphasize repentance as a condition of receiving God's great mercy. Some prayers and hymns offer a simple, more celebratory assurance of the divine mercy we die into, emphasizing that we are already completely safe in the arms of God, and that Christ's redemptive will for us is far more spacious than our own imperfect acts of repentance. We see such a reminder in the seventeenth-century Dutch hymn that begins "There's a wideness in God's mercy like the wideness of the sea," and later reminds us that "the love of God is broader than the measures of the mind."

Surely the broad reach of God's mercy is the deepest kind of comfort any of us can offer those who are facing death. And all these petitions and assurances still inform our hopes for "a good death." Naming some of those hopes may help us focus the prayers and the practical support we extend in the days and weeks of helping someone we love prepare for death.

*Hope for forgiveness.* This is a time to offer and receive forgiveness, releasing each other from lingering resentments. Forgiveness may involve naming old offenses or hurts, though sometimes naming them can reawaken them in ways that don't help. A simple intention to release each other from anything that impairs the love between you, anything that might prolong guilt or resentment, and even from the need to understand the sources of old conflicts, can open both your hearts to peace. I have often marveled at Cordelia's words to King Lear, who had rejected and disinherited her. When at the end of his life he asks her forgiveness, acknowledging how much cause she has to hate him, she immediately responds, "No cause. No cause." By all rational measure she indeed has cause to despise him for his selfishness, vanity, and folly. But in that moment, her heart is so full of gratitude for reconciliation and so flooded with the love she has longed to give and receive that there is simply no room for resentment. That scene offers rich material for reflection on the way forgiveness transcends all scorekeeping.

*Hope for completion.* This is a time, as common counsel often suggests, to "take care of old business" and "set your affairs in order." Still, one of the most consoling words I heard in a recent funeral service was that, though the stories of our lives on earth are completed at death, all deaths, even those that come at the end of a long, full life, leave some sense of incompletion. Perhaps that sense remains because we are created for eternity, and time belies what we most deeply know about ourselves — that our lives are not completed here. Nevertheless, longing for "a sense of an ending" is deeply human. So one practical gift that can help bring "a good death" to a loved one is to help achieve the particular completions — small and large — that release the mind from earthly concerns. These often have to do with paying debts, distributing gifts and mementoes, recording untold stories, expressing hopes for children and grandchildren, destroying old letters or other documents that might cause pain, and giving a final gift to church or charities — matters for which we might offer a helping hand. Each completion can open more space in the mind and heart of our loved one to rest more fully in peace.

*Hope for what can happen only in solitude.* Many who have been surrounded by attentive family and friends for weeks and months before death finally die — perhaps by choice — when no one is around. Some spiritual work requires solitude. Acceptance, trust in the processes at work in body and spirit, deep release of fear, and rest — these all require a time of inner and outer quiet. It is not unusual to hear a person who is dying admit the burden of having to comfort those he or she is leaving, having to meet the social expectations people bring to the bedside, and having to endure not only his or her own pain but the pain of others' grief. Helping protect periods of solitude, even short ones, can be a gift we give the dying — at least the offer of quiet time in which they may learn how to "let goods and kindred go, this mortal life also."

There are other things to hope for at the time of death: a last conversation with an estranged friend; the encircling arms of a beloved who knows how to hold without hurting; music that opens the heart and speaks of heaven; and stories whose endings invite the dying to imagine the heavenly banquet, the marriage feast, the home that awaits us all at the end of this journey. If it is our task and privilege to be caregivers in these precious hours and days, then our work is to open hospitable space and time for what needs to happen, to recognize particular needs as they arise. Our role is not to second-guess or manage, but to pray for the grace to release our own agendas and walk with the dying one, step by step, taking each turn in trust.

*We ask you, Gracious God,*
*for the grace of a good death for* _____ ,
*and for us, who follow:*
*for forgiveness and a will to forgive,*
*for completion of what is left undone,*
*for life-giving solitude when it is needed,*
*for spacious and hospitable hearts*
*where your Spirit can dwell*

*and finish the good work*
*that you began at birth.*
*Bless and comfort this beloved child of yours,*
*and lead him/her home*
*in perfect trust and perfect peace.*
*Amen.*

# Things of the Spirit

*To set the mind on the flesh is death, but to set the mind on the Spirit is life and peace.*

ROMANS 8:6

Paul didn't pull any punches. One might imagine ways to be a bit gentler about our very common tendency to "set the mind on the flesh." I don't believe Paul meant we should treat the very fleshly lives we were given with contempt. I do think he meant for us to recognize that with every thought, with every movement of the heart, both the dying and those who are living on have an opportunity to choose life or death. So, like the writer of Deuteronomy, he urges us therefore to "choose life" in much larger terms than are possible when we think only of life in this particular form in this particular place on earth.

Part of our ministry to the dying is to help them choose life in this broad and hopeful sense, and to gently offer opportunities to reflect on "things of the spirit."

A friend of mine with aggressive fourth-stage cancer remarked with more bemusement than anxiety, "When I get up in the morning, I don't know whether my job is to work on ways to keep living or on ways to die well." Because she got to live her dying, as those who die suddenly don't, she knew she had choices to make about where to put her remaining energies. It was in conversation with the friends who shared hours at her bedside that she developed a practice of dwelling in that paradox — a practice that enabled her to live her final days with a sense of humor and sustained interest in the details of this life going on all around her while also making ready in increasingly evident ways for the great transition to come.

Paul's phrase "things of the Spirit" lends itself to broad interpretation: one can pray, read Scripture, seek wisdom in stories of saints, pay attention to the reassurances, grace, and guidance that come, unplanned, in dreams and conversations. As companions of the loved one on his or her final journey, we can reflect together on the metaphors that help us take stock of life as it has been given and is being taken away: life is a journey; life is a race; life is a blessing; life is a battle; flesh is grass; God is light.

We can also share laughter, even in the face of death, swapping odd memories, recalling amusing encounters, and enjoying a little irreverent irony about hospital food. In Wendell Berry's energizing poem "Mad Farmer: Liberation Front," where the "mad farmer" offers a list of ways to live well in the face of the forces of death, he includes the simple imperative "Laugh" at the end of a line whose beginning is "Expect the end of the world." It's a striking juxtaposition: those of us who really accept and practice life as saved and immortal beings "get the joke." Death looms large, but the primal curse diminishes into something truly, deeply laughable, shrivels like the witch in *The Wizard of Oz,* in the light of minds informed by and practiced in the simple understanding that our way here leads us home.

The poem ends with this oft-quoted injunction: "Practice resurrection." It's another phrase that invites a spectrum of interpretations. At its most theologically straightforward, it may mean to live into the fact that the resurrection has already taken place, and to claim and remember that truth in the hardest times. It may also mean to practice a habit of mind that recognizes even the most ordinary moment as a bit of eternity and seeks not duration but a depth of "now-ness" that prepares us all for the full and final experience of now that we call heaven. It is not a place, or a time, but a way of living the days we get — even the last one.

*Even now, Lord, let us help one another choose life. Let _____ live this dying in confidence and emerge from this darkness into your marvelous light. And help us who remain in this world for a time to be reminded when we think of _____ to consider those "things of the Spirit" that put all our days in divine perspective. Amen.*

# Hoping Against

*Death undoes us less, sometimes, than the hope that it will never come.*

PICO IYER

Right now some old and dear friends of mine are keeping vigil, as we talk together, with their young daughter, who, by all accounts, is dying of a cancer that began in her carotid artery, metastasized to her lungs, and from there to her spine, kidneys, and other parts of her slight body. She is beautiful. They are beautiful. Another friend who joined them for a couple of days reported that the house, where siblings and extended family were gathered, was full of singing, prayer, and even laughter. "The prognosis was very hard," her mother wrote, referring to one doctor's prediction that her daughter would die within two weeks (it has now been three). "But," she continued, "there have been moments of real joy in these days."

The more illness and dying I witness, the more I believe that a core characteristic of suffering, including the suffering of grief, is complexity. Its emotional chemistry is never simple; if suffering were to be represented by anything physical, I think it might be a protein — long, intertwining strands like a tangled necklace — or a Celtic knot that, in Wendell Berry's words, makes a design the eye can "follow but not know." Deeply felt, richly experienced, and courageously faced, dying is likely to include those moments of joy my friend named (at the risk, no doubt, of being misunderstood by those who deal with grief by reducing it to one gray thing). It will also very likely include searing physical pain; a sense of loss; fear; shame; fatigue; peace; grateful remembering; bemusement; curiosity; compassion for those whose lives are disrupted by the intrusive presence of one's suffering self. My job as witness to all these things in these hard days is to honor the ways each of those feelings comes as an invitation or challenge or respite to the dying and to those who keep watch.

Suffering and dying fully entered into, as Pico Iyer suggests, may be less devastating than the fear, avoidance, and resistance that, though futile, sap our energies just when we need them most. "She will die" or "She is dying" may be paradoxically life-giving messages to the anxious self, bringing a truth into full focus that re-organizes everything — our choices, our priorities, our expectations, our fears, our hopes.

That last — hope — rides on its own paradox in seasons of death and dying. Only when hope of continued physical life is laid aside can other kinds of hope flourish. "Hope of heaven" may be a phrase that has lost its power to awaken for some; "heaven" is one of many biblical words that has been flattened and trivialized by thoughtless use. But what remains for the one for whom we keep vigil is hope of transformation, of life in a new dimension, freed of this failing body and suffused with light, "dignified, invisible,/Moving without pressure," as T. S. Eliot imagines the presence of beings embodied more lightly than we. I cling to this hope as I watch the precious body before me dwindle day by day.

I remember vividly the simple assertion of a woman who spoke years ago at a memorial service for a mutual friend, once a professional dancer, who had died after years spent in a wheelchair because of multiple sclerosis. "Kathy has been liberated," she said. "She is dancing now." Suddenly the image of Kathy emerging from the constraints of her unreliable flesh into a leaping delight of quickened senses (to borrow again from Eliot) and surging energy brought me a moment of reawakened faith in the gift of life we are promised. "Today you will be with me in Paradise," Jesus says to the "good thief." Only a breath more or less, a thin strip of time, a veil easily torn separate us from that altered condition we call "eternal life." C. S. Lewis depicts it as a state of more solid reality in one book, but in another invites us to imagine creatures who live at another frequency, to human eyes as evanescent as the light that changes when clouds pass.

We have only promises cloaked in metaphor to help us imagine the next life, but those promises are a sound basis for hope — those and a mercy that is "from everlasting to everlasting." So letting go of the loved one who is dying challenges us to stretch our hope, not to the breaking point, but to the tipping point Julian of Norwich reached when she realized with complete conviction that "All shall be well, and all manner of thing shall be well."

*God of all Hope, lift us out of hopelessness into trust. Teach us how to hope even in times of loss, and what to hope for. Plant in us, we pray, a seed of hope for the life you have promised, where each of us may be united with the communion of saints and with all those we have loved, all those who have loved us, all whose lives are linked to ours by birth, baptism, and circumstance, in ways you alone know. Help us to live this hour of death, and the hours of our own deaths, filled with a hope stronger than grief, knowing that your love is stronger than death. Amen.*

# Things Take Time

*I can't*
*Know her now. There's no time.*
*Smell of camphor, dust of bromide.*
*The bed stanchioned with perpendicular silver rods.*
*. . . all her extensions tied up*
*And abstracted. The tongue frays*
*at the edge of the sentence,*
*the fingers at the hem of the sheet. . . .*

JIM SCHLEY, "HER STROKE"

We don't want to see those we have loved in this condition. We don't want to see their radiance, their laughter, their quick intelligence, their various moods, their capacious, imaginative, inimitable selves wracked by pain and reduced to the terms of such visible need. The paraphernalia of hospital or home palliative care can seem not only unfamiliar and invasive, but offensive. For some it can be an unnerving distraction from the kind of communion one hopes for in the final hours.

We all live with the two-edged tools of medical technology. They serve us, sometimes save us, and sometimes seem an unwelcome imposition on a process that might be gentler and kinder without them. Few of us will escape the complex end-of-life decisions that come with a range of options available. Wanting "what is best," we are sometimes at a loss about how to discern what "best" might be.

So when we are faced with those decisions for a loved one, it is a time to pray for ongoing guidance. It is a time to pray for clarity about what "enough" looks like, for deep attunement to the needs and wishes of the one whose dying has brought responsibilities we neither sought nor want. It is a time to pray for the courage to assume the responsibilities that are ours, to share them generously with others equally involved, to inform ourselves, to sign papers, to speak with medical staff when we might rather be in a quiet place attending to our own sorrow.

There may be grace even in the unwelcome details of filling out health-care forms and preparing meals and managing medical equipment. Though they are frustrating and distracting, these things may also anchor us to the ordinary in ways that help us act when grief seems almost paralyzing. They may also give us access to others' compassion in surprising ways and places. A staff person may emerge from the margins with a cup of tea and blessing at just the right time. If we're in a hospital room where others take care of the tubes and tape and paraphernalia, we may find that a quiet, scrub-clad nurse practitioner brings a certain calm when she enters the room, and wonder if we are "entertaining angels, unaware."

If we accept that teachers will be sent to us on our journeys when we need them, and we look for them, we will find them even at this ending. There are those who can help us with the very human, demanding work of caring for our dying loved one. The spiritual care may not come from the chaplain, or real comfort from the assigned nurse, but if we open ourselves to guidance through this narrow passage into safe harbor, guides will come. Sometimes a relative who rarely visits will show up at just the right time. Or a conversation overheard in the hallway will open a new avenue of reflection. Or a doctor on call — not our loved one's doctor — may bring a fresh way of speaking about what is happening that utterly reframes it. An e-mail from a friend long since "lost," who has heard and cares, may drop into the moment as an unexpected gift. The constellation of family, friends, and strangers often shifts dramatically in a time of illness and dying. Some find themselves emotionally ill-equipped and back away. Others move in from the margins to become key players in the last scene, bringing practical skills, good humor, sharp discernment, deep experience, or simply kindness.

None of this is lost. The Amish, I have read, regard those who are sick and dying as gifts to the community because of the love they bring forth. It may be that the role of the person making ready to die is to provide an axis around which love may gather and flourish. We never fully know what deep purposes we are serving, and when life may seem most purposeless, as it often does to those who are ready to die, it may be serving purposes of which none of us are fully, consciously aware. Even in the midst of our own sorrow and pain, and that which we are witnessing, some good work may be coming to completion. May we, as attentive and loving caregivers, allow it scope.

*Loving Creator,*
*you made us for your own delight*
*and for purposes we cannot fathom.*
*Help us, in sickness and in health,*
*to serve those purposes faithfully,*
*in trust and in patience,*
*until you call us home. Amen.*

# Untimely, Unseemly

*Why is light given to him who is in misery,*
  *and life to the bitter in soul,*
*who long for death, but it comes not . . . ?*

JOB 3:20-21

I was surprised one day when I asked my mother, not long before she died, how she was — an ordinary question on a rather ordinary day. She looked up, patient, a little puzzled, and replied, "Well, I'm fine. I just can't figure out why I'm still here." She was ninety-four at the time, not really fine, though not terribly ill, suffering the slow ravages of congestive heart failure, and not lost in dementia, though the confusion that overtook her occasionally was a source of distress to us both. She didn't have a "death wish," but she was ready to go.

Several times in those last months I found myself gently reminding her of the call to wait on the Lord, of the fact that our times are in God's hands, of the fact that simply being human and here has its goodness, despite her deepening feelings of uselessness.

Many have much harder final acts than hers. Some are in

severe, intractable pain. Some are lost in the shadowlands of dementia, fearful, anxious, suspicious, and agitated. Some sink into depression. Denise Levertov's disturbingly honest poem "Death Psalm: O Lord of Mysteries" challenges readers to come to unflinching terms with the bitter fate of outliving oneself, in lines like these that describe a woman who had "made ready to die" with grace and courage, but then lingered far beyond the end she had hoped for:

> She did not die, but lies half-speechless, incontinent,
>     aching in body, wandering in mind
>     in a hospital room.
> A plastic tube, taped to her nose,
>     disappears into one nostril.
> Plastic tubes are attached to veins in her arms.
> Her urine runs through a tube into a bottle under the bed.
> On her back and ankles are black sores.

The poem ends with a prayer any of us might pray at a wrinkled bedside where someone we love has lain too long — an outcry to the "Lord of the mysteries" about the cruelty of "laggard death" that "steals/insignificant patches of flesh" but fails to take the one who waits to be taken. The speaker is Job-like in her acknowledgment of a God whose ways are not only inscrutable but sometimes sorely trying to body and spirit.

Providers of palliative care and hospice workers are trained to honor the business of dying, to focus, however long the process, on care, comfort, presence, and support. Their task is not to hasten death, but to help those who are ready to go gently, and those who are not ready to prepare. When all pretense of "cure" has been relinquished, there is good work to do. For the dying, the work might lie in offering simple breath prayers, acts of gratitude or acquiescence or trust, repeated phrases that center the mind and open the heart, and receiving the blessing of touch and song, forgiveness and prayer. Those to whom it is given to die consciously have choices to make about what final gifts to impart, how to honor their own deepest needs and the grieving of those they love.

Not everyone gets a satisfying exit. Most deaths are not what we might call "timely." But when there is time and awareness, much can happen. I have seen long-postponed forgiveness asked for and received in the final hours. I have seen those facing loss come together as a family in new, life-giving ways. I have seen evidence of encounters with invisible others that seem more like vision than hallucination. We know only a small part of what work is happening subtly, below the level of intention or awareness, midwifed by angels.

We don't know what preparation is taking place, but we can trust that all of us — the dying and we who care for them — are being prepared for an end and a beginning. Preparation is very different from pointless, prolonged waiting. What it requires of us is not to strive, but to allow. To say yes, and then yes again until all speech stops this side of the thin veil that separates us from the kingdom of heaven, which is always near.

*You who healed men and women who waited,*
*bring our waiting to a gracious end.*

*You who called us into life,*
*Call _____ into the new life you have prepared.*

*You who stood patient before your torturers,*
*give us patience as you make us ready for this going.*

*You who brought us safe into this world, and have seen us*
    *safely through thus far,*
*bring _____ safely home*
*in your perfect and appointed time.*
*Amen.*

# *Walking the Valley*

*Even though I walk through the valley of the shadow of
death, I will fear no evil, for you are with me; your rod
and your staff, they comfort me.*

PSALM 23:4

This most familiar of biblical assurances about death serves as
both a declaration of confidence and a prayer for confidence
in a fearful time. Even people of great faith are not immune
to fears about the great transition we face when we cross over
into a place or condition even the best theologians can only
imagine. To witness that transition is a teaching like no other.

The rod and the staff are the shepherd's protection against
lurking dangers and implements for keeping the sheep safe
and near until they reach the fold. They are comforting precisely because the dangers are real: physical pain, exhaus-
tion, and anguish that extinguish all desire to pray; spiritual
desolation; demons of guilt, bitterness, anger, and of fear itself. These afflictions may well come to the dying, and seem
overwhelming.

More than one pastor I know has remarked on how often

the dying ask to hear the Twenty-third Psalm. They are in that valley, alone in ways that human company cannot fully dispel, but often more open to divine presence than ever before. The Shepherd walks with them, and we who sit with them in solid flesh by their rumpled beds can remind them of that by speaking these beloved words when they are most needed. Even if the mind strays, even if the heart sinks, even if the body tires and falls into restless, unwelcome sleep, nothing, "neither death nor life . . . nor any other thing," can separate these loved ones, who seem so quickly to be slipping away, "from the love of God in Christ Jesus" or from the reach of the Shepherd's staff.

Despite many marvelous stories about near-death experiences, most of which testify to a healing light and a joyful welcome that lie just beyond the veil, we can't have the kinds of certainty about death that Western minds are conditioned to want — palpable, conclusive evidence of safe passage and happy outcome. What we can know is that "I will be with you always" is a promise to claim for ourselves and for those with whom we keep vigil, as one companion goes and another stays, as a parent releases a child to God, or a child her parent.

The final line of Wordsworth's sonnet to his daughter, "God being with thee when we know it not," offers a similar reminder that we are held, surrounded, watched, accompanied, and loved whether or not we recognize divine presence. The simple reminder that the Psalmist offers in the phrase "for you are with me" is a plain statement of fact as much as a profound statement of faith or of hope.

I have never read or seen *Hamlet* without finding myself

particularly moved by Horatio's parting words to his dying friend: "Good-night, sweet prince, and flights of angels sing thee to thy rest." Death is a time to remember the angels, too — quiet messenger presences too subtle for our senses, but at work in the world, and witnesses of our journeys and of their endings. It helps me to imagine that they sing the dying on their way, and that the path through the valley of the shadow is lit with song.

The dying are preparing to enter into the company of angels and saints. *The Book of Common Prayer* is explicit about this: included among the petitions for a death vigil is this kindly hope: "May angels surround him, and welcome him in peace." In that vision of hospitable embrace, the shadows of this valley lift, and we are reminded of the heavenly banquet foreshadowed in every celebration of the Eucharist. Dying may take minutes, or months, but it moves those whose turn has come toward a safe harbor, a fold, a family, a "condition of complete simplicity," a banquet, an embrace, a house of the Lord where they will be welcomed home. All these images are invitations to rest easy and rest assured, in this hardest of times, that weeping will indeed endure for a night, and that joy will indeed come in the morning.

*May flights of angels sing her to her rest.*
*May she be welcomed even as she is mourned.*
*And may our mourning not turn to bitterness or despair,*
*But be threaded with hope, even on the darkest days*
    *to come.*
*Amen.*

# Confession

*For what we have done and left undone . . .*

ANGLICAN CONFESSION

I have always appreciated this deceptively simple phrase from the Anglican prayer of confession that covers such a wide spectrum of sins, omissions, mistakes, and unfinished business. Each of us will die with things left undone that we ought to have done, and very likely with some awareness of "things ill done and done to others' harm/which once you took for exercise of virtue." T. S. Eliot's candor in reminding us that we sometimes remain unrepentant because we mistakenly think we've been doing good is especially useful as we examine our consciences and seek authentic forgiveness. A gift that may lie even in final hours laced with pain is the opportunity for confession to be heard and assurance of forgiveness offered.

I did not grow up in a tradition where formal confession was practiced or encouraged. We were urged to repent and follow Jesus, but were not taught to kneel and say words that made that repentance explicit and public. Those words, I later discovered, were words to grow into. To read prescribed acts of confession was to shine a broad light on what needed for-giveness. It took me a while to recognize that repentance and contrition don't leave you drenched in guilt, but rather free you from it. Every week, still, I need and am grateful for the moment in the liturgy when the priest or pastor offers some version of this compassionate word: "Friends, believe the good news. In Jesus Christ you are forgiven." It is a statement of fact and an assurance of something accomplished. It offers needed relief from self-blame.

That we are forgiven is good news. In my experience, those facing death need to hear this news. Two dear people I re-member had similar anxieties about having carried anger toward their parents for years. They breathed more easily as we talked about God's complete forgiveness, mercy, loving-kindness, and eagerness to welcome even the most prodigal sons and daughters.

If there is time, it is good to allow for words of confession and forgiveness at the time of death, not because they are nec-essary, but because they are freeing. They often help the living, and they let the dying approach that great transition lightened and unburdened, with nothing impeding the centripetal force that draws them homeward.

When our daughter learned that it was time to stop treat-ment and receive palliative care, she gave her own clear-headed consent to that decision. Almost immediately after-ward she turned to her dad, who stood close at the bedside, encircled him in a deep hug, and said, "I'm sorry, Dad. I'm sorry for everything." It was a simple, clear, uncomplicated act of confession, love, and completion. It brought a strong, complicated relationship to a gracious conclusion. What they both needed was given and received. There were things done and left undone. Our daughter laid them down and went her way, also leaving behind a blessing for her father.

Sometimes it's as simple as that. Sometimes it happens with the help of clergy. Sometimes it happens in solitary conversation with God. But it may fall to us who sit with the dying to serve as their confessors. Though absolution is not ours to give, assurance is. Those moments are a time to invoke the priesthood of all believers, and to hear generously and assure confidently that God's own promise of forgiveness will not fail.

*God of all Mercy, we ask your forgiveness for all we have done and left undone, for all that remains unconfessed and unrecognized, and for amends not completed and not to be completed in this life. In your grace, supply what we owe you where we cannot or have not made right our wrongs, for your Son's sake. Amen.*

# Blessing

*This is the blessing that Moses, the man of God, gave to
the people of Israel before his death: . . . all [God's] holy
ones are in his hands.*

DEUTERONOMY 33:1-3

In many cultures it is the privilege and duty of a dying el-
der, when possible, to confer a blessing. Though it may seem
strange to think of the dying as having duties to perform,
to recognize that they still have something to impart to the
community is itself a matter of blessing for everyone con-
cerned. When family and friends gather at the bedside, it is
not only to offer but to receive comfort, and something more
than comfort.

Blessing is much more than affectionate leave-taking. It is
an exercise of power and an act of faith. In traditional cultures (as in the case of Isaac's blessing Jacob), it often signified
transfer of property, conferring material benefit and social
authority, but also spiritual benefit. When we invoke God's
blessing on others, we become conduits of God's own grace
and step into the priestly role that all believers may assume.

It can be appropriate and empowering to ask a person who is dying to bless those who remain. As the dying prepare to enter a new dimension of life with God, they are in the process of leaving behind all earthly things and relinquishing earthly relationships. To seal with a blessing the stories that each of those relationships has shaped accomplishes several things:

1. *Forgiveness.* The Roman Catholic sacrament of confession begins with the penitent's words: "Bless me, Father, for I have sinned. . . ." A blessing lays the guilt to rest, and opens the way for whatever reconciliation or reparation needs to happen. For some of us, that forgiveness may be a crucial part of our healing after the one we loved, but wronged, has died. All of us wrong the ones we love. All of us remember moments we wish we had lived differently. If those we have alienated die without reconciliation, grief work is that much harder. To ask for a blessing is humbly to acknowledge both one's own need and the power of the other to meet that need. To receive blessing is to be released from all that inhibits the free flow of love.

2. *Encouragement.* A blessing extends generous approval and permission to follow one's own path without fear of damaging the relationship. When a parent blesses the marriage of a child, the act signifies full acceptance and recognition of a fundamental change in their relationship. So when a person who is dying blesses those left behind, it may be received as a gift of encouragement to choose life, to let go, to complete their own journeys with joy.

3. *Protection.* A blessing invokes God's protection on the one blessed. Especially if the person dying is a parent, a final

prayer that the children one is leaving may be protected from all that might blight the spirit, from overweening grief, from temptation to despair, from debilitating depression, and any other danger that might beset the newly bereaved may be a real and practical help for both the person leaving and the person left behind.

4. *Gift.* May there be a seed of gift in this loss. May good gifts come even in a dark time. May your heart remain open to receive what gifts remain, and what gifts are still to come. In all these ways, a blessing is both a reminder of and an imparting of a gift to the one who so needs to be equipped with hope and consolation for the days to come.

You may recall that when Jacob blessed the sons of Joseph, there was some confusion about priority of heritable rights. Let's not kid ourselves about the petty competitions, jealousies, fears, and other complex emotions that complicate leavetaking. The goodness of blessing, when it can happen, is that it cuts through those things to the heart of the human story: we are here for a time, and for a time are each other's, and then we move into another dimension, another frequency, another "place," and join the wide communion of saints.

We need release from each other, and from all that binds us to earthly contracts, in order to continue our respective journeys. A ritual of blessing may not insure that release, but it can invite all those at the bedside to open their hearts, even if they are breaking.

*Bless us even now, Lord.*
*Protect us as we walk into the darkness,*

*guide us as we navigate the challenges we face,*
*sustain us in our sorrow,*
*comfort us in our beloved's absence,*
*teach us to endure loss with grace,*
*remind us of your unremitting love.*
*Hold us close to your heart.*
*Amen.*

# In a Place Apart

*Sometimes . . . it took him several seconds to bring himself back to the present. He could see they thought his mind was failing; but it was only extraordinarily active in some other part of the great picture of his life — some part of which they knew nothing.*

WILLA CATHER,

*DEATH COMES FOR THE ARCHBISHOP*

Willa Cather's representation of a dying man's state of mind may be imaginary, but it offers rich food for reflection on the process of dying. She reminds us that just because the dying person is not "here," we need not assume he or she is nowhere. Rather, the dying one may be fully occupied with inner work that needs his or her attention.

Like childbirth, dying is a kind of labor. It may be taking place at a soul level. It may be taking place in the inner reaches of the mind, where old memories, scenes that need to be revisited and set to rest, are more real than the physical present. Even what we call dementia, in our accustomed haste to assign clinical terms to complex conditions of the body, mind, and soul, may involve good and necessary work. Often aging persons with dementia believe that their parents are waiting, that their children are actually siblings, and that they need to catch a bus. All these "delusions" are resonant with the reality of preparation for departure and for encounters with others long dead.

Those who are dying are preparing. They are relinquishing. They are reviewing and remembering — literally seeing again and piecing together in a new way episodes in a life rapidly coming to its narrative close. They are coping — with pain, regret, loss, interferences, confusions, and perhaps even unwelcome visits from well-meaning family and friends. They may be enjoying old movies from their memory banks. They may be imagining, or praying, or receiving messages and guidance. They may be resting by still waters or wandering along a new path. They may be troubled about unresolved matters only they can work out for themselves. They may be musing, or even amused — quietly chuckling over ironies the rest of us don't recognize. There are many active verbs here, all of which suggest that we shouldn't be too quick to think that when our beloved one is staring into space or at the wall, nothing is happening.

We don't really know. That may be one of the hardest things to handle as we keep vigil by the bedside: we just don't know, and can't know, what is being accomplished in the quiet and solitude of dying. Death is a mystery. Theologians and neurologists and psychologists and family members and colleagues can go only so far; there is a holy of holies in each of us before which a veil is drawn. There is a part of us known only to God.

Our work, while those who die are doing their work, is to "hold them in the light" — to pray for a merciful and gentle passage, to be available, to honor their process, and to accept the solemn privilege of bearing witness to this unique enactment of the one task given to us all — to come into this world for a time and then to leave it, letting God take the measure of our days and assign whatever meaning they have. The rest, as T. S. Eliot puts it, "is not our business."

*Source of all knowledge and all mystery,*
*give us peace in our unknowing.*
*Still our insistent curiosity*
*and let us stand humble before the mystery of this*
            *great transition,*
*trusting always that your grace is sufficient*
*and your mercy beyond imagining. Amen.*

# Readiness

*I warm'd both hands before the fire of Life;*
*It sinks; and I am ready to depart.*

WALTER SAVAGE LANDOR,
"DYING SPEECH OF AN OLD PHILOSOPHER"

"Men must endure their going hence even as their coming hither: ripeness is all," King Lear realizes. Landor's simple declaration, "I am ready to depart," testifies to that ripeness, which many who face their own death come to with realism and tranquility. It can often be the case, though, that those who provide attentive, watchful, loving care, and who in the process are trying to cope with imminent loss, aren't nearly as ready as the person dying. The one who is dying and the one who witnesses are engaged in very deep and very separate kinds of preparation — one to leave this life behind, the other to continue it in a season of experiencing painful loss and sorrow and finding the courage to heal.

A friend who had faithfully attended to his wife as she lay dying recounted later that he had said to her as she labored to take her final breaths, "It's okay to go"; he had learned that sometimes permission can help the person relax into release without struggle. "But even as I said that," he recalled, "I thought, *It's NOT okay. It's not okay with me for you to die. It's not okay for you to leave me here alone. It's not okay for this to be happening.*" She was ready; he was not. It took a long time for him to be "okay" with what life had dealt the two of them.

Dying takes time. Grief often takes longer. Both processes take inner work. Honesty with yourself about what is truly inevitable, the courage not to grasp at straws of false hope, the generosity to let go when everything in you wants to cling and resist — none of these things comes easily or naturally to most of us. And up to the day of death, we may not feel ready.

But the fact is, we may be ready, even when we do not feel that way. The Spirit that groans within us with sighs too deep for words also works within us to prepare us for what must come. We never fully know what we're being prepared for, or at what level preparations are taking place. It is certainly not all a conscious process, and certainly not entirely under our control. But in the hours of dread and sorrow that may threaten our peace of mind and even our faith as we await a death we long to postpone, we are being made ready for the next stage of our journeys, whatever those may be. Our hearts will be broken open, and that openness will make way for a new source of light, for a new level of reliance on grace and guidance, for life-giving help from unexpected places, for the companionship we'll need on this hard stretch, for the solitude that is larger than loneliness and holds within it seeds of restoration.

Readiness isn't just a feeling, but a soul state. That may seem a little glib, but it is also true that we can assume we have what we need to meet what must come and cannot be avoided. We have grace sufficient for the moment. Our job is to recognize that grace in the many forms in which it is offered, and accept it with gratitude, however much our hearts long for a different gift, a different outcome, a different life story. The story we inhabit is larger than any earthly life, and the outcome promised well beyond our imagining. To hope for things unseen may seem almost unthinkable in the darkest hours, but it is a hope that can steady us even in the reeling momentum of events we would give our lives to change. "Thy will be done" is one of the hardest prayers to offer. But it may be the only one that will get us to real readiness for what God gives.

*Lord of Life and Destroyer of Death,*
*make me ready for what must come.*
*Give me peace that passes understanding*
*and a patience larger than my resistance.*
*Help me to help the one I love prepare for leave-taking,*
*and help me bear this loss with generosity and hope. Amen.*

# Release

*There is a place of full release, near to the heart of God.*

CLELAND BOYD MCAFEE

Often sung at funerals, "Near to the Heart of God" was written by Cleland McAfee in response to the death by diphtheria of two of his young nieces, and sung for the first time outside their quarantined house. I heard it many times, growing up in a church where faith in God's nearness and trust in God's promises were in some ways at their liveliest when loss came to one family or another. The line that struck me as a child and continues to strike me with particular resonance is the one quoted above: "There is a place of full release, near to the heart of God."

That full release can be imagined as both the release from the hard things of this life for the person who is dying, and the full release required of us who have to let them go. Releasing them into God's hands, where they will be held near to God's very heart, seems a much more manageable task than simply releasing them. Abstractions simply don't work at a time like this.

Christian tradition offers a variety of ways to approach death. It is the primal curse, result of the "happy sin" *(felix culpa)* that "merited such a Redeemer." It is a transition into a new life in and with Christ (though denominations differ about the nature of that transition and its relationship to the day of Christ's return) and with the communion of saints who have gone before us — that wide, variegated swath of humanity that includes many unlikely characters. It is a time of judgment and of mercy when we will "know even as also we are known." It is a time of separation between the dead and the living and also of reaffirmation of the life in Christ that finally nullifies that rending moment.

McAfee's word "release" is a reminder of Paul's assertion that "for me to live is Christ; to die is gain." To die is to be released from an arduous journey, perhaps filled with all manner of earthly delights, but also, and increasingly, a journey in a dark and precarious valley. Those who have died are released from the profound anxieties that come with chronic warfare and economic instability, climate change and failing schools and dwindling aquifers and insufficient health care. To enumerate the ills that flesh and the earth are heir to may seem cold comfort to us who will continue living here a while longer, but it can also help to soften the feeling that death is disaster. The other side of loss is release from suffering.

We suffer what we must in this life, and suffering is part of our learning. Suffering can breed wisdom, although, as an old friend — a Holocaust survivor — pointed out, suffering does not necessarily ennoble people. It can make them petty and selfish and bitter. Suffering is not in itself a virtue or a good to be sought, though when it is inevitable, it can be an occasion for exceptional grace. We can "offer up" our sufferings in union with Christ's sacrifice; we can find in them an inducement to greater empathy with others and allow them to open our hearts. We can, like women in labor, breathe through the pain, observe it, ride it, reframe it, and sometimes escape it. Most of us, most of the time, would choose that last option, both for ourselves and, perhaps more urgently, for those we love, whose suffering can at times be almost unbearable to watch.

A mother I know who spent months trying to help her child survive aggressive cancer and almost equally aggressive treatments told me that in the final few days her prayers changed from asking for her daughter's healing in this life to asking simply for her release from her suffering. It's an excruciating prayer for a devoted parent to pray, but realistic, both in terms of its acknowledgment of the limits of this body and this life, and of its implicit trust that there is a place of full release that is, and will be, good.

There is a time to pray for that release, as there is a time to pray for healing. Those prayers are not mutually exclusive. Healing may come as a reprieve from death but also may come in death. As we face the loss of someone we love like life itself, we may not know when to pray for what, but no prayer is wasted. God, who knows our needs and knows our deepest purposes better than we do, honors our prayers for healing and will bring each of us to a point of "full release," in this life or the next.

*From our addictions and anxieties,*
*Giver of Life, release us.*
*From disabling physical pain,*
*Giver of Life, release us.*
*From sins that bind us and temptations that distract us,*
*Giver of Life, release us.*
*From sorrows we cannot ourselves assuage,*
*Giver of Life, release us.*
*From all fears that darken our hearts,*
*Giver of Life, release us.*
*From all resentments, bitterness, anger, and confusion,*
*Giver of Life, release us.*
*From our sufferings in this world, when they no longer*
        *serve your purposes,*
*Giver of Life, release us. Amen.*

# Like a Seed

*The kingdom of heaven is like a grain of mustard seed. . . .*

MATTHEW 13:31

Heaven has been trivialized and sentimentalized in movies and children's books, and at the hands of artists who deal mostly in pastels. When death is near, thoughts naturally turn at some point toward heaven. All of us who are facing death — our own or another's — may find ourselves browsing through a thick file of images, stories, and phrases about life after death in an effort to deal with the anxieties that accompany the preparation for the transition from this life to the next.

The Gospels and Christian tradition offer a wide range of ways to imagine the "kingdom of heaven," most of them more mysterious than explanatory, all of them inviting us to approach its mystery with hope. As we sit in the shadow of an impending death, it can be helpful to reflect on these, gleaning gently some of the insight and consolation and challenge they offer as we find ways to help someone we love prepare to go to the place prepared for us all.

Each of the metaphors for the kingdom of heaven — a concept not confined to the afterlife, but also about the depths of the present — offers comfort as well as insight. The kingdom is like a seed that carries a promise of huge, varied, continuing life within its tiny compass. It is like a field of wheat where weeds are allowed to grow and from which the wheat will be harvested. It is like leaven, working in silence and time to make ready what has been prepared. It is a treasure to be discovered and claimed. It is a gathering and a wedding feast. No single image is entirely sufficient. Together they invite our imaginations to stretch to the edge of what imagery can convey.

We have the wisdom of saints and theologians to help us reconsider and reframe our notions of heaven when they dwindle into the banal or simplistic. In one of his finest sermons, Jonathan Edwards left lavish testimony that "heaven is a world of love." St. Catherine of Siena's assurance that "All the way to heaven is heaven" underscores Jesus' teaching that the kingdom of heaven is among and within us — a declaration that thins the partition we imagine between this life and the next. Desmond Tutu offers this cheering reassurance: "We may be surprised at the people we find in heaven. God has a soft spot for sinners. His standards are quite low." And C. S. Lewis foreshadows it in *The Last Battle,* where a character cries, "I have come home at last! This is my real country! I belong here. This is the land I have been looking for all my life, though I never knew it till now." That heaven is our home is probably the deepest, most comforting truth we can claim when we find ourselves facing terrible feelings of abandonment as the one we are losing prepares to "go there."

Despite the many good words we've been given about this great mystery, we are still left in a cloud of unknowing. To hope for heaven is to practice radical trust that what awaits each of us is a great and good thing, prepared in love and promised in mercy beyond the reach of human imagining to children of a Creator who made us for himself, and gave us restless hearts designed first and last to find their rest in him.

*Heavenly God, bring your child home,*
*healed and safe in your arms.*
*Teach us a hope of heaven*
*that will assuage the sadness of being left*
*on an earth made colder*
*and darker by this dying.*
*Bring us home at last to the place*
*where we belong. Amen.*

# Consent and Consolation

*God does not leave us*
*comfortless, so let evening come.*

JANE KENYON,
"LET EVENING COME"

Good poems can often serve as prayers. Many good poems are written as prayers, worth keeping close in hard times for the help they offer in speaking for us when words are hard to find. Jane Kenyon's powerful and memorable poem "Let Evening Come" models the way acceptance can lead to empowering assurance. It reads at first like a litany of acquiescence or permission, every line or two beginning with the curious word "Let." The opening stanza suggests an acute and palpable sense of how time wreaks its changes, and how those changes are not all diminishment, but rather an exchange of one form of beauty for another:

Let the light of late afternoon
shine through chinks in the barn, moving
up the bales as the sun moves down.

The opening words "Let the light" evoke God's "Let there be light" in a way that echoes God's creative action in Kenyon's own consent to what is and must be. The several stanzas following reiterate that consent as they slowly take account of nature and the creatures in this world doing what they do — the fox, the cricket, the dew, the wind — offering a prayer that is both concession and command in a repeated "Let" that acknowledges the many ways life intersects with death, day with darkness.

In the final stanzas, as in so many of the Psalms, the speaker turns to face the reader directly with a word that is both directive and prophetic, fraught with a certain urgency even in its calm assurance that evening will come: "Let it come as it will, and don't/be afraid." Again and again wisdom traditions underscore this word of instruction as a way of liberation — do not be afraid. "Fear not" is followed often by a promise like the one the angel gives to Mary — "for behold, I bring you tidings of great joy" — or like the promise the poet gives here: "God will not leave us/comfortless." The line break after "leave us" doubles the effect of the assurance: God will not leave us. And God will not leave us comfortless. Both promises are true, both to be claimed and counted on in the moment of loss.

In light of that promise, the final words ring with a new level of acceptance or readiness. The poem, a prayer, expunges the boundaries between the physical and the spiritual dimensions, invoking perhaps the oldest image of death, the end of day. But in the Jewish tradition that harks back to Genesis 1: "and the evening and the morning were the first day." Evening is both an ending and a beginning. Sabbath begins at twilight.

Though the poem makes no mention of the joy that comes in the morning, the quiet hope in the double negative of the last stanza, "God does not leave us comfortless," is enough for now, Kenyon suggests. Both the one dying and the one left will have what they need. Neither may fully know what that need is until, quietly and surprisingly, it is met.

*Teach us to accept what we cannot change.*
*Teach us to receive each day as a gift, including the last.*
*Teach us to rejoice in unlikely moments.*
*Teach us how to release those we love with gratitude*
*and faith that in their dying they are born to eternal life.*
*Amen.*

# WITNESSING:

## STORIES OF LETTING GO

*These few anecdotes about encounters and insights that have come in or near the hour of death, collected from a number of witnesses, may encourage us to enter those hours with hope, deepened respect for the mysterious process of dying, trust in the work of the Holy Spirit and of the human spirit in the course of that transition, and awareness that the living, the dying, and those who have died are linked in ways we can barely imagine. Though these stories come from various people, I have told them all anonymously and in the first person, trying as faithfully as I can to render them as they were told to me. Some are my own.*

~

I was spending the night in the room where my father lay in a hospital bed, giving my mother a much-needed night of uninterrupted sleep. Around two in the morning, after weeks of immobility and profound weakness, Dad suddenly sat up, smiled, and started vigorously applauding. After a minute or so, he lay back down and sank back into sleep. This was a few days before he died. The hospice nurse laughed when she heard about it, and simply said, "He was in a good place." That surge of energy and visible delight remained an encouragement and a consolation to me during and after his death; I am convinced he was getting a little peek beyond the veil that was soon to be lifted.

Our daughter, who loved to dance, lay in a sunny room in the palliative care unit of a hospital, letting morphine ease her pain and waiting for the slow shutting-down of her body and consciousness to take its inevitable course. Family members rotated in, keeping vigil. She floated in and out of awareness, though we all suspected she was more aware than she seemed, and we spoke to her on that assumption. As her kind, handsome cousin stood by her bedside, she suddenly opened her eyes, smiled at him, waved her hands gracefully in the air, and said, "Last dance." The sweet humor in her remark as well as the clear awareness of her impending departure gave us a new respect for her independent decision to stop futile treatment and for her complete acceptance of her own early death.

~

I sat with my dying father, talking with him a little about how he felt, about his medications, and — first in oblique ways, then more directly — about his dying. We fell into silence for a few minutes. Then he commented, with a look of mild amusement, "This is so interesting!"

~

I am not Roman Catholic, nor is my friend, whose Polish father-in-law lay dying in her home. Though he had lived for years in England and married an Anglican, his English remained uncertain and his Catholicism as unchanged as his Polish syntax. "I wish we could pray with him in a way he could hear and recognize," my friend said wistfully. "I don't know Polish," I replied, "but I can say the rosary in Latin, which is what he would have learned as a child."

Delighted at the suggestion, my friend found his rosary and handed it to me. I knelt by his bedside and, with a prayer that my prayers might be received by a loving God who translates all our efforts to pray rightly, I began: *"In nomine patris et filii et spiritus sancti . . . Pater noster, qui es in coelis, sanctificetur nomen tuum . . . Ave Maria, gratia plena, Dominus tecum. . . ."*

By the time I'd repeated three or four *Ave Marias*, it seemed to me he had visibly relaxed. Saying the rosary also brought me into a state of surprising peace that simply held me in a sweet prayer space for the half hour or so that it took.

My friend's father-in-law died later that day. My friend was grateful for those prayers, but I much more so. I felt I'd been blessed with a gift of intimacy and grace in having been invited into that moment and given the opportunity to accompany this dear man from a far country on a step of his journey home.

∼

My stepdaughter, who had never found it easy to accept me, or her dad's marrying me after her mother's death, lay wakeful and restless on what was to be her last night of intermittent consciousness. It was my turn to lie in the hospital room near her. My blankets were thin, the room chilly, and her breathing loud and troubled, so I lay awake, praying, imagining, remembering, and wishing for another blanket. Suddenly, after a number of semi-audible words I was unable to understand, she said clearly, and with what seemed a ringing tone of recognition, "Mom!" I had no doubt she was seeing the mother she had so missed, and I felt a thrill myself in being a witness of sorts to that encounter.

A bit later, to my greater surprise, she just as clearly called out my name. I rose and went to her side, took her hand, and said, "I'm here." She stretched out her arms to be held, so I got in bed with her, and she turned and clung to me like a small child, smiling more fully than I'd seen her do for many months. I don't know how long we lay there in that embrace, but I basked in gratitude, listening to her breathing quiet down. Finally, just before she drifted off, she said, "I love you."

It was her last gift to me, and one that had been long in coming. I'm not sure whether she knew it was me or thought it was her mother, but in either case I was touched and honored to receive those words — a last clear act of love before she let go — whether on her mother's behalf or on my own didn't seem to matter. Indeed, it seemed to me her words joined the two of us in having completed the assignment of mothering her in her often difficult journey here, and I trusted that I was handing her back to a woman whose love would be continued and perfected in the larger realm where they were about to meet again.

~

My mother had been in and out of consciousness for several days, "actively dying," as hospice people identify that slow transition. At one point, since she seemed to be wanting something, reaching upward toward something, I leaned over her bed to speak with her and see if I could discern what she might need. Her eyes were wide open, and she seemed deeply engaged in watching something (or someone) just behind my shoulder. I leaned in closer, saying, "I'm right here, Mom."

But it wasn't me she wanted to talk with: with an effort she rearranged her head so she could see just past me, and reached out again to someone I couldn't see, with a look of eagerness that made me poignantly aware that she was already being welcomed by others. Not wanting to interfere, I stepped back and watched while the encounter continued for a few minutes. Afterwards she lowered her arms and sank into a peaceful sleep.

~

The morning our daughter died, my husband and I sat with her for a while. Then we called the other kids one by one to let them know. One of them called back, a note of amazement in her voice. "Mom," she asked, "what time did she die?"

"Around 8:15," I answered.

There was a pause. She went on: "You know how B likes to bounce around on our bed in the morning. Well, right around that time he stopped, looked at me, and said, 'Mama, Auntie S is happy.' That was just before you called." Another pause. "He must have known."

Later that morning, in the midst of preparing to come see us, she called again. "Mom," she said with similar amazement, "B just asked me where I was going. I said I was coming to be with you. I didn't say anything about S or her dying. He walked across the room, took my hand, and said, 'Mama, Auntie S isn't sad anymore. She's all done.'"

It was the word S herself had used only days before when the doctors had told her that they could pursue further treatments, but that in all likelihood they would be painful, expensive, and futile. She said with remarkable calm and clarity, "Don't do anything more. I'm done."

She knew. And then he knew. Their clarity has been a consolation many times in the months since her death. That a two-year-old could be such an open receiver and transmitter of information not yet spoken from sources beyond our range of awareness gives new dimension to the call to become like a little child.

~

Days before his death, though he was physically debilitated, mostly nonverbal, and sleeping a great deal, Dad was alert and responsive to those of us who floated in and out of the room, reading to him, bringing ice chips, praying, and sometimes just quietly talking with one another. At one point, three of us — a daughter and two granddaughters — stood together at the foot of his bed. He gazed at us and, strangely, a little to one side of us for a while. Then, with a look I could only identify as amusement, he raised a hand, pointed at each of us in turn as if counting, and then held up four fingers.

Someone else appeared to be there with us. I hope and imagine it was an angel or a visitor from the great communion of saints, or Jesus himself, coming to greet a quirky and eccentric but good and faithful servant. I thought of the line from "The Waste Land" where T. S. Eliot reimagines the disciples on the road to Emmaus. One of them asks, "Who is the third who walks always beside you?" Someone was walking beside us, beside him, then, and very likely someone is now — inconspicuous, unannounced, quietly accompanying us with no need for anything from us but to listen in now and then for the still, small, subtle voices that lead us on our way.

# MOURNING

# In It Together

*We die with the dying:*
*See, they depart, and we go with them.*

T. S. ELIOT, "LITTLE GIDDING"

In the final days of her life, my mother's moments of lucid-
ity became less frequent, her hours of sleep more prolonged,
and her breathing slower. In the hours I spent at her bedside,
the words "going away" and "receding" and "withdrawing"
kept coming to mind. Though I was with her in what seemed
moments of profound intimacy, I also felt the space between
us widening as she moved closer to the threshold she would
soon cross without me.

It is not uncommon to hear people say after the death of
a beloved person, "Something in me died when he died," or
"When she died, I died a little, too." The accuracy of those
observations reaches beyond metaphor. In *Lament for a Son*,
Nicholas Wolterstorff writes, "I buried myself that warm June
day. It was me those gardeners lowered on squeaking straps
into that hot dry hole. . . . It was me over whom we slid that
heavy slab. . . . It was me on whom we shoveled dirt. . . . It was

me we left behind, after reading psalms." The truth in that insistence is visceral, not figurative. Loss is not the same as death, but in very real ways we do "die with the dying."

Their deaths remind us, for one thing, that all flesh is grass, and that every day moves us closer to our own earthly ending. At a time of loss, this reminder can be strangely comforting. Whatever our lives may be like in the next dimension, as believers we share the conviction that we are homeward bound. This is not a death wish, but a fact that sustains a hope that sees through the fear of death.

For another thing, we *are* part of each other. The lives of those we've been given to love are grafted to ours in ways that make us interdependent, sharing not only the nourishment of meals, conversation, and memories, but the alignments that allow us in some precious moments to recognize that our common lives, made of earth and spirit, draw us into a oneness that is utterly real. So when John Donne proclaims "No man is an island entire of itself," he finds his elegant way through several lines of metaphor to his ringing and famous conclusion:

> Any man's death diminishes me,
> because I am involved in mankind.
> And therefore never send to know for whom
> the bell tolls; it tolls for thee.

The death of one you love is your death, too — to bear with, to witness, to release yourself into, and to emerge from, changed. In death as in life, in learning from love of neighbor about love of God, and in watching our "neighbor" die, we are offered those hard gifts of grace through loss that come with our common lot. We are joined to all those who mourn even as we remember that we will be mourned in turn, and make that passage which leads us to the cloud of witnesses who hover so thickly around us, filling the very air we breathe with their compassion.

Nothing will be the same again. Life continues, and grace and eventually laughter and even joy if we seek the resilience that faith and friendship provide. But as surely as we have to let go of the one we loved and walk away, finally, from the bedside, we have to let go of that part of ourselves that was shaped and animated by his or her presence and let ourselves be bent by the wind of the Spirit to new and modified purposes. It is perhaps good not to drive ourselves too quickly to reassurance; there is a time to mourn as surely as there is a time to die, and we need not foreshorten it. The heart may need to break before real healing can happen. Randall Jarrell's surprisingly candid insistence on giving sorrow its due may be helpful when pious clichés do more harm than good: "Pain comes from the darkness/And we call it wisdom. It is pain."

Nevertheless, people who believe in the risen Christ know that if the pain cannot be assuaged for a time, that time has an end, and that end is a new beginning. The one who is leaving is embarking.

*Giver of all Gifts, help me to hold even those I most cherish with an open hand. Let this loss not diminish me, but break open my heart and teach me what I need to learn*

*— that all life is yours, that death is not the end, that you will find us and bring us home. Help my grief to melt into gratitude in due time, and teach me complete reliance on your holy will. Amen.*

# Gone

*He is not here, but has risen.*

LUKE 24:5

I was thirteen when my grandfather died. He went in a way we might all wish to go — after a long, rich life and vigorous old age, without any illness that he knew of. Having celebrated my brother's birthday in the evening, read the evening paper, and bid everyone good night, he walked out to the backyard cottage he shared with my grandmother and slept until he took his last breath.

I woke after midnight, when I heard my father on the phone to the coroner: "I think my father has died." My first response was not grief so much as amazement. Though I had been to funerals and heard much about death from the four candid adults I lived with, I was still young enough to feel that somehow those four adults occupied unassailable places in my personal landscape. I didn't get out of bed, but waited until our mother came to wake us kids up, tell us what had happened, and then, surprisingly, ask if we wanted to see Grandpa's body before the coroner came.

Mom had been a missionary in South India, where death was pervasive and public. She had helped clean bodies for burial and held those near death until their breathing ceased. While I wouldn't say she had, like St. Francis, made friends with "Sister Death," her faith was informed by a clinical practicality and unabashed curiosity about the life of the body that gave her an ease many don't have in the sickroom.

On this night, she held our hands as we walked down a short, dark pathway into the cottage and went, tentatively, to the foot of the bed. Grandpa's craggy face looked shockingly white and unfamiliar, though I knew every line and whisker. For the first time I was struck by a simple thought that has recurred at other deathbeds since: *He is not there. Death is not sleep. He is gone.*

The words are simple. The physical fact is as mysterious as anything we ever encounter. Even the quietest, most natural, most "timely" death comes as a disruption because we are created to live. The longing to keep living has driven people to "heroic" interventions, some beyond the limits of reason and resources. Faith that life does go on — that this life is only one chapter or one dimension of a much fuller life — can soften our resistance and infuse our grief with hope. But even to the most devout, death can feel like a radical insult to our deepest sense of how things should be.

*He is gone.* It is not a flat fact, but a startling echo of the angel's words to the women who came to Jesus' tomb: "He is not here, but has risen" (Luke 24:5). When death comes, what is living in us departs. A long, frank look at death may help resurrection hope take deeper root. When "He is not here" is a clear, present, palpable fact, we may come to terms with two biblical claims: "Behold, all flesh is grass," and "I say to you, this day you will be with me in paradise."

Heaven has been trivialized by movies and greeting-card pieties. Our work as believers in times when loss threatens to overwhelm trust is prayerfully to seek a renewed and deepened hope of heaven. Not more explicit assurances about what it will be like — speculations that most often lead to empty argument — but a stronger conviction that, as physicists discover new dimensions, so we can broach the mystery of life's departure from the body with an intelligent awareness that the eschatological "there" and "then" of heaven need not be tied to time and space, but may point to an instant translation into a new dimension. That the veil between this life and the next is thin, that the testimony for life beyond this body is ample, that the promise that this passing is not the end of the story — these are assurances that we need to retrieve from the realm of cliché and claim as "sure and certain hope."

The loss remains, and in this life is absolute. The one we loved is gone, but. . . . There is a second clause to that sentence which makes all the difference.

*Holy Spirit,*
*You dwell within us and among us.*
*Deepen our hope of heaven.*
*Make that hope sure and certain,*
*sturdy and resilient.*
*Come like wind and lift us into a wider life.*

*Come like fire and ignite our appetite for the life we are given.*
*Come like a still small voice to comfort us in these hard times.*
*Amen.*

# Our Common Lot

*How shall I speak of doom, and ours in special,*
*but as of something altogether common?*

DONALD JUSTICE

In the judgment scene of Robert Bolt's *A Man for All Seasons,*
when Sir Thomas More is about to be condemned, More inter-
rupts the glowering judge who opens his thundering speech
with the word "Death . . ." and quietly finishes the sentence
for him: ". . . comes to us all, my lord." The reminder is startling in its simplicity. We all die. That truth deserves its own
sentence before we add a "but" clause to object to the cruel,
unjust, or untimely ways people die, or to protest from our
deepest places of pain against the particular death that looms
in our own lives with a shadow so heavy it feels impenetrable.

Doom, as Donald Justice says, is our common lot. Perhaps
the only comfort in that observation is the fact that we are
not alone, though the feeling of aloneness can be intense and
relentless sometimes. Enduring the dying of persons we love
so fiercely we can't imagine life without them — that suffering lies in the profound sense of isolation in our particular

loss. Placing ourselves in the wide communion of saints and sinners who have died, are dying, and will die can offer some consolation. We all get a turn.

To remind ourselves that death comes to us all, that it is our common lot, that it is the inevitable end of our earthly journey isn't to insist that it is to be welcomed as a blessing. The biblical story line opens with the fall into death as the primal curse. Even if we believe that Christ has conquered death, that it has lost its sting, and that for some, like Paul, "to die is gain," we can still rightly lament our losses.

At a memorial service some time ago, when a friend's life was being commemorated with much celebration, a Jewish woman sitting next to me asked with some bewilderment, "Don't Christians mourn?" We do. We must. We should. To mourn is to open an avenue of the particular grace and blessing promised in the Beatitudes. To mourn is to open ourselves to comfort, which is a unique dimension of love. To mourn is to make our sorrow hospitable to those who are willing to enter into it. It is possible to mourn generously by allowing our sorrow to awaken others to their own unmourned losses. It gives loss its due and allows our broken hearts the time they need to heal. Perhaps the Jewish custom of rending garments would be an apt and helpful "outward and visible sign" of mourning that needs to be entered into fully and bravely before it gives way to celebration.

No one can dictate exactly how much time that healing takes. Sorrow recurs in surprising ways, sometimes many years after loss. But the social dimension of loss — the fact that we are in it together and called together by it — gives our communities the right and the obligation not only to support us in our mourning, but to call us back from it into the life that is left for us and help us learn to live it on new terms. In dying, as in living, "it is not right that man should be alone."

Most of us get a few chances to approach that threshold as witnesses before it is our turn to cross it. We know that the only way out is through. We know that new life awaits us all, and that Love will bid us welcome. But this knowledge doesn't, for most of us, entirely offset the very human rage and sadness that cry out against the incompletion and brokenness of the lives we live now. Our work is to accept the sorrow, to live it, to suffer it, and finally in humility to let it be drenched in the healing waters of love that come to us from as many sources as we allow — great wells of it, great waves of it, and daily infusions from old friends and from strangers who may be angels sent to walk us through the valley of the shadow.

*Loving God, you send them and we entertain them,*
  *unaware.*
*Teach us to welcome their heavenly companionship.*
*Show us how to come alongside those who weep,*
*and to lighten sorrow by sharing it.*
*Teach us the ministry of presence.*
*Let our words not break silences*
*in which your voice may be heard.*
*Thank you for every hour we have together.*
*Keep us both, the living and the dying, close to you*
*when our earthly pathways part.*
*Hold us both, as you hold us all,*
*in the hollow of your strong and spacious hand. Amen.*

# *Permission*

*There is no judgment here.*

STAFF COUNSELOR AT A HOSPICE HOUSE

The week before our daughter died, we took her to a hospice house. Six patients' rooms surrounded a large living area where family could gather, look out into the garden, read, sleep, prepare meals, talk, weep. There was a quiet room where we could rest. Counselors were available. The staff gave us a kindly welcome, assuring us that they would take care of our daughter's physical comfort, and that we were there to do whatever we needed to do as we kept our hard vigil. "There is no judgment here," one of them said. "People grieve differently. Do whatever you need to do. If you need to talk with a staff person, just ask. Eat. Talk. Sit by her bedside as long as you like. Watch football if you want to. No one will think less of you if you give yourself a break."

We were completely touched by all that gracious permission, and I realized how perfectly it allayed anxieties I hadn't realized I was carrying about how to go through the difficult hours we were to spend in the limbo of those last days.

In seasons of grief I have been surprised by how many people seem to believe there is a "right" way to cope with loss — appropriate behavior at the bedside and the memorial service, emotional propriety in the aftermath, timely recovery after a prescribed season of sorrow. The traditional year of wearing black did serve to allow space and protect the bereaved, and to summon them back into community so as not to encourage obsession with sorrow. Still, that year is too short for some, too long for others. Elisabeth Kübler-Ross's five "stages" of grief, while helpfully descriptive, can be misapplied as a measure of whether one has adequately "completed" a particular stage before entering another. Stages and other schemata may help us tease apart some of the tangled strands of feeling that thread through our dreams and our days. But grief is generally messier and less predictable than that.

The most helpful books I've encountered on the process of grieving are personal accounts. They give us windows onto others' grieving that remind us that even this loss, unlike anyone else's, is also a shared experience. C. S. Lewis's *A Grief Observed* is a classic of its kind. Lewis wrote it in the weeks after his wife's hard and painful death, and it rings with an authenticity that enriches and complicates the scholar's characteristic clarity. We see in what seem fairly raw descriptions of his states of mind an awareness of dividedness from self that is something different from the utter anguish of the first wave of loss: "I not only live each endless day in grief," he writes, "but live each day thinking about living each day in grief." He tries out analogies to get at the character of loss: "The death of a beloved is an amputation." Grief is a dentist's drill that drills on, "whether you grip the arms of the dentist's chair or let your hands lie in your lap." And each analogy opens a new avenue of reflection. Finally, he realizes, grief is not a state but a shifting, subtle process in which nothing "stays put": "One keeps on emerging from a phase, but it always recurs. Round and round. Everything repeats. Am I going in circles, or dare I hope I am on a spiral?"

We can't map it when we're in it. That disorientation is part of the experience. There are islands of laughter. There are "normal" days followed by very dark ones. Anger and gratitude, lassitude and fits of energy come unbidden and unwieldy into our waking lives and sleep; what is a refuge and respite on some nights is on other nights a site of demanding dreams.

What we can know is that these are ills that all flesh is heir to. That grief, like love, has "a thousand faces." That though we may never "get over it," we may heal, and that healing will likely come in ways we can neither predict nor control. The joy that "cometh in the morning" will come like the morning, in its own due time, a gift and a summoning back to the journey that remains to be completed.

*God of all comfort, help us find comfort even in the hard tasks of this season — the caregiving, the waiting, the preparing, the grieving. Help us to accept what comes in due time without hurry or fear, and to accept your gracious permission to address our own needs along the way. Amen.*

# Immortal, Inexplicable

*Why should a dog, a horse, a rat, have life,*
*And thou no breath at all?*

KING LEAR

In the first days following the death of one you love, the sounds and sights of life going on its rattling way in the streets and stores and even in the pews of churches can seem offensive. One woman I know protected herself from going to parks and other places where she might see children the age of her child who had died; seeing other children alive and well and happy was simply too hard. King Lear's heartrending cry over his young daughter's body is a cry of outrage at what seems simple injustice — some seem to "deserve" life more than others. Especially when a young person's life is cut off, when people in what seems to be their prime are stricken with terminal illness or lose their lives in auto accidents, it is natural to wonder why — when they had so much ahead of them, so much to give, so much still to learn — their stories stopped in what seems like mid-trajectory.

One of the hardest things to grasp about God's justice is

that it is not about human deserving, or measured by human notions of merit. The Psalmist's frustrated question "Why do the wicked prosper?" is much like King Lear's: gifts — even the gift of life itself — seem not only inequitably but irrationally distributed.

The question may seem irreverent, but we have to ask it in order to grow into answers that are bigger than our projections. If we are too quick to resign ourselves to unquestioning submission, we may miss the kind of wisdom that comes in so many biblical stories from wrestling, challenging, even badgering the Almighty for answers. God's answer is always relational — trust me, follow me, wait with me, believe in me — or personal: "Where were you when I laid the foundations of the earth?" "I am who I am." It is the kind of answer parents give small children incapable of receiving explanations. They hold them and say, "I know. I'm here."

• One of the best explanations of trust I received in my younger years was this, from a friend who seemed particularly able to trust against the grain: When you really trust someone, you don't trust them to do or not do certain prescribed things; you trust that whatever they choose to do, even if it looks unreasonable, is grounded in good will and good judgment. So we may also assume that God's ways are grounded in grace.

And what we know about grace is that it often emerges in darkness, flowers in dry places, and takes us by surprise. A momentary lifting of the weight of grief, a dream in which all is well, a line in the day's lectionary, an old hymn we find ourselves humming that offers new awareness, a phone call from one who knows how to listen from the heart, an acute

awareness of the kingdom of heaven that is "near at hand" —
these are just some of the ways answers come — not to answer
the question of why, but to meet our great need.

*Holy One,*
*immortal, invisible,*
*unresting, unhasting,*
*teach us to trust in your inexplicable ways.*
*Deepen our hope for a heaven*
*we can hardly imagine.*
*Appease the pain of loss.*
*As our hearts break, keep them open.*
*Widen our compassion for the many*
*whose losses also seem unbearable.*
*Make them bearable.*
*And help us to bear them with patience and grace.*
*Amen.*

# Grief that Keeps Going

*How long must I take counsel in my soul,*
*and have sorrow in my heart all the day?*

PSALM 13:2

Sorrow can seem endless. It turns us inward, making every ordinary task burdensome and social contact unappealing. It covers our waking hours with ash and makes sleep troubled and unrefreshing. It is isolating and lonely. The Psalmist's cry "How long?" reflects what we may well feel on a deathwatch — a loss of relationship to ordinary time with no sense of an ending and nothing to wait for.

A description of these feelings may sound like clinical depression, but sorrow isn't the same as depression; it is a completely appropriate response to immeasurable loss. In the words I have come to love from the old *Book of Common Prayer,* there are times when mourning and sorrow are "meet and right." There is "a time to weep." We need that time. The question the Psalmist raises is how long that time is. In Ecclesiastes it is a "season" — a term that seems reassuring in the way it offers full permission to grieve and implies that there is a natural limit to grieving.

"How long" will depend both on what we are given to endure and on how we manage it. We may need to dive deep into it before we surface. We may need a time of complete withdrawal from ordinary duties and encounters. Good bereavement counselors give those of us who mourn generous permission to enter into our grief and explore its depths before we require of ourselves or of those who share our loss that errands be run, letters answered, meals prepared.

On the other hand, we can get stuck in our sorrow. Its on-and-on-ness can become a habit. Like any other disposition, it can disconnect us from the healthy correctives that community provides, and inure us to the comforts available in prayer, meditation, Scripture, and worship. Because chronic melancholy is a danger to which authentic sorrow makes us vulnerable, every cultural tradition makes some provision for community participation in mourning. Our sorrows are never simply our own business. Precisely in those "hours of lead" when we feel least inclined to seek others' company or to pray, we need the moorings that keep us connected to the solid ground of earthly occupations, family, friends, and even work.

Most cultures recognize a period of mourning during which special provisions and allowances are made for people undergoing the first emotional ravages of loss, and those periods have endings — the seven days of sitting shivah, the three months thereafter, the year of wearing black, the cycle of anniversaries when strong waves of bereavement may rise up and crash again with undiminished pain. Those external benchmarks remind us, even in the midst of emotional fluctuation, that there is a time to return to the lives we are given, bereft and still subject to deep currents of sadness, but obedient to the summons to choose life in the very wake of death.

Sometimes that obedience may feel like no more than empty ritual, where "the feet, mechanical, go round," to borrow Emily Dickinson's apt and accurate image. But it may be that getting to our feet is all we need to do. When we are sinking in the quicksand of sorrow, we may need to allow ourselves to be guided into new pathways by those who love us and also by the One who leads us beside still waters.

We can count on that guidance. Others whose turn has not yet come, or who have survived the worst passages of mourning themselves, can see horizons that are obscured by the fog of grief. And even if it feels, day after day, that no answer to the question "How long?" is forthcoming, we have reason to hope. We can hope not only for the joy that "cometh in the morning" but also for repose (even before that joy dawns) in the arms of the One who promised to be with us always — in our sorrow as in our joy, to the end of the world, and to the end of our own journeys as we wind our way home.

*Jesus, Man of Sorrows,*
*acquainted with our grief,*
*meet us in our sorrow.*
*Bless us in our mourning.*
*Bless us in our pain.*
*Bless us in our parting.*

*Let our grief not turn to bitterness.*
*Let our sorrow not isolate us,*
*but open our hearts to all who are sorrowing.*

*Lead us beyond restless questioning to trust.*
*Lead us through our dark imaginings to hope.*
*Lead us back from our rebellion to a faith*

*made sturdier by sorrow.*
*Hold us in the night while we weep*
*until we are able once again to rise up into morning*
*and receive your joy. Amen.*

# *Comfort*


*It is Margaret you mourn for.*

GERARD MANLEY HOPKINS,
"SPRING AND FALL"


Sorrow can be confusing. You feel it in your belly, in muscles that grow heavy, in the effort it takes to breathe. Though you may know what it is "about," deep sorrow has an encompassing quality that grows to include more than the immediate loss. New grief brings up old grief. New seasons bring around again the anniversaries and memories that shape and shade the liturgical year. In "Spring and Fall," where Gerard Manley Hopkins addresses a young child in her sadness, he acknowledges this quality of grief, both in the final line, "It is Margaret you mourn for," and in another simple reminder: ". . . no matter, child, the name:/Sorrow's springs are the same." Death is a reminder of our own mortality, and of loss as a part of "the blight man was born for."

However, the truth Hopkins tells about the scope of sorrow comes not from a person of little faith, but from one of great faith. In his own struggle with sadness, he wrote poems whose range of truth-telling — about the grandeur of God that charges the world, and about dry roots deep in the self that beg for rain — has offered a hospitable place of respite for millions of believers whose pain drives them to the edge of doubt. The ancient question of how a loving God can consign us to agonies of suffering and loss arises even among the most pious in the midst of agony. Prayer, company, or even occupation with ordinary things can lead us back from the edge that question takes us to, but we know the edge is there.

The old hymn "How Can I Keep from Singing?" includes the insistent lines "No storm can shake my inmost calm/while to that Rock I'm clinging . . . ," which acknowledge both the storm and the place of calm. The word "inmost" is key here: the inmost place is like that place where we are knit together in our mothers' wombs — secret, even from her whose heartbeat introduced us to the rhythm of life in this world. It is like the "heart of my own heart" we sing of in the hymn "Be Thou My Vision," alluding to a place deep in our own hearts where the Spirit of God dwells, mysterious, wholly intimate, wholly other. Grief can and should drive us to those inmost places where the only real comfort lies.

"What comfort do you receive by trusting in God's providence?" the Presbyterian study catechism asks — a question that lies docilely on the page among the others that line up for our consideration, but that burns itself into memory when we most need an answer. The answer we read in that short volume may be more sufficient than it looks — that God "watches over me each day of my life, blessing and guiding me wherever I may be," and that, entrusting myself to God's care,

"I receive the grace to be patient in adversity, thankful in the midst of blessing, courageous against injustice, and confident that no evil afflicts me that God will not turn to my good."

These are large propositions. They are generous promises. The catechism offers them as statements of fact, without apology, without modification. In the simplicity of their matter-of-factness, they may be carried like smooth stones in the pocket, fitting the shape of our clutching hands: *I am watched. I am blessed. I am guided. I receive the grace I need. Good will come, and God will come, even in the very midst of suffering.*

*Come, Lord Jesus.*
*Come, Holy Spirit.*
*Come, Creator God, who knit me in my mother's womb*
*and brought _____ into my life.*
*For the gift of _____ 's life, I give you great thanks.*
*In the sorrow of his/her leaving it, I ask for your comfort.*
*Be my rock and my hiding place.*
*Be my shelter in this storm.*
*Grant me the grace to complete my own journey*
*as so many have before me.*
*Amen.*

# Those Who Mourn

*Blessed are those who mourn, for they shall be comforted.*

MATTHEW 5:4

Mourning opens time and space for sorrow. It can also foster wisdom and generosity. In one of his stories about an old man rescued from impersonal institutional care by a family who want to bring him home to die, Wendell Berry contrasts the sterilities of the hospital with "the larger, looser, darker order of merely human love." Human love takes us into dark places where we are taught the hardest things. Those we love suffer, and as we love them, we suffer with them. Ultimately we lose them. The hard work of love is to see each other through, in sickness and in health, and often unto death. We can't mourn what we haven't loved. Those who mourn are those who love.

Those who mourn are blessed because they are members of that "larger, looser, darker order." They have traded in self-protection for the pain of authenticity and brokenness. They have traded in control for trust. They have traded in the false comfort of self-pity for God's own comfort, which comes most richly to those who open their aching hearts widest. The Beatitude above is worded in the plural, suggesting that mourning, as distinct from private grieving, is a community practice: to mourn is to join with others in the sorrows that beset us all, and to recognize in our own grieving an occasion to remember the communion of saints who have made this journey before us and who make it with us in a generation beset by agencies of death.

That others are enduring comparable pain doesn't lessen our own, but to remember their pain in our own darkest hours is to practice a costly generosity that drives out bitterness. Mourning like this — inclusive, imaginative, and open-hearted — does not harden into anger or wither into pettiness. In his small, stirring book, written after the sudden death of a beloved son, Nicholas Wolterstorff offers this reflection on who Jesus may have meant when he blessed those who mourn:

> Who then are the mourners? The mourners are those who have caught a glimpse of God's new day, who ache with all their being for that day's coming, and who break out into tears when confronted with its absence. They are the ones who realize that in God's realm of peace there is no one blind and who ache whenever they see someone unseeing. They are the ones who realize that in God's realm there is no one hungry and who ache whenever they see someone starving. They are the ones who realize that in God's realm there is no one falsely accused and who ache whenever they see someone imprisoned unjustly.

Those who mourn are blessed because their hearts are made sturdier and more capacious. A young friend of mine who lost his mother while he was still in high school continues after many years to find solace in the line she passed on to him from Kahlil Gibran: "The deeper . . . sorrow carves into your being, the more joy you can contain." Gibran goes on to ask, "Is not the lute that soothes your spirit the very wood that was hollowed with knives?" Sorrow makes a space that at first may seem only a gaping, open wound, but can, even as wounds do, become the site of healing. I've known a number of people who have found healing for years-old conflict with family members in mourning them; death incited them to deeply re-evaluate and radically reframe the life stories of those who died, and see them in a new light. This can happen in surprising ways at funeral services, in the midst of sorting through possessions left behind, in conversation with others who knew them in a different context.

Perhaps the most paradoxical of the Beatitudes, and the most challenging, this pronouncement of blessing upon those who mourn brings its own gift of comfort. Mourning itself is a blessing. Taking time to mourn, gathering with others who grieve, re-imagining life and hope in new terms, entering into conversations that drive us deeper into reflection and on into prayer — these acts of mourning bless us as we consent to them. May we consent again on every gray morning of our grieving to let ourselves be blessed.

*Bless us now, Lord, in our mourning.*
*Grant us the rest we need, the trust that will sustain us,*
*and what healing may come in this hard time. Amen.*

# Like a Leaf

*Walk around feeling like a leaf.*
*Know that you could tumble at any second.*
*Then decide what to do with your time.*

NAOMI SHIHAB NYE, 1990

I write this on the evening of a young woman's death. She was twenty-five. She was lovely, and much loved. She fell like a leaf — gently, lightly, before the season had time to change. Cancer took hold of her whole slight body, wrapping itself around organs and arteries. She had time to exchange a great deal of kindness, encouragement, and affection with the many who cherished her before she quietly took her last breath, surrounded by a family at prayer. Her Facebook pictures show (as many do) a life full of fun and friends. I'm sure there were shadows here and there behind the hugs and laughter. But she seems to have done well with her time, and to have been capable of giving and receiving joy, even in her last weeks. Her death is yet another reminder — particularly sharp, as the deaths of young people always are — of the truth that our time here is temporary. None of us knows how temporary —

not the one I care for, whose dying seems so imminent, nor I myself, though I imagine my length of days still to be long.

Being completely present to the present moment is a habit of the heart taught and encouraged in every tradition I know of — taking no thought for the morrow, considering the lilies, bringing the full force of loving attention to what presents itself on our path. It is, like so many "simple" practices, hard. We do look ahead and back. We have to, in order to do the good things in the world we are called to do. The challenge is to live in time without abandoning the timeless now, which is where we learn to be citizens of heaven. Now is my time to care for. There will be a time to be cared for. We take our turns.

So how do we remain in the moment when other things constantly tug at us? Being in the moment is illuminated by the simple analogy of tennis instruction: you are taught to anticipate, run to meet the ball, and return to center after each hit. The "return to center" is key. The center is the grounding point. The present moment is where we retrieve our balance, strength, and orientation, again and again. Dancers know this, and surfers and skateboarders. The life of the body teaches us about the life of the spirit.

But the body is an instrument on loan. We receive it, live in it, with it, by it, know what we know by means of its five senses, and finally let it fall like a leaf when it is time to move into what T. S. Eliot calls "another intensity." Our freedom lies in obedience to the way of all creation — to live into the seasons we are given; to rise, crest, and ebb; to consent to the terms of time for the duration of this journey; and then, as Mary Oliver so memorably and simply writes, "when the time comes to let it go,/to let it go." One of Wendell Berry's short poems, now a song, is also a prayer for the openness to the moment, even the moment of death, that enables us to live fully into the short lives we are given without fear of their ending:

And when I rise
let me rise up
like a bird
without regret,
joyfully.

And when I fall
let me fall down
like a leaf
without regret,
gratefully.

Gathered around the bed of a dear friend when he died, a number of us who loved him sang this song again and again, making it our tribute to one who had lived and died in a spirit of complete acceptance of the terms he was given. He had engaged in courageous resistance to nuclear arms and oppressive policies, but his personal life was simple, kind, and receptive. "Like a bird . . . like a leaf . . ." — simple lines asking for gratitude, blessing, trust in living and dying.

The natural world can teach us a great deal about how to live, how to die, and how to witness others' living and dying. We can learn from other creatures how to accept what is given, flourish in working with what is given, and die in due season. Many creatures die "unnatural" or "untimely" deaths, cut down by accidents or toxins or careless machines. Many of us have died or will die in similar ways as well. But to see how acceptance may extend even to that — to living with joy the life we are given, through all its losses, and dying with gratitude when our moment comes — is to find our place in the mysterious order of a universe graciously fashioned and shared, and to find our way into the promise that "in life and death, we are the Lord's."

*Let _____ , and let me as well,*
*rise and fall, Lord, in your good time,*
*like a bird, like a leaf,*
*borne on the breath of the Spirit.*
*Amen.*

# A Season of Separation

*Neither death nor life nor principalities nor powers nor*
*things present nor things to come shall separate us from*
*the love of God which is in Christ Jesus.*

ROMANS 8:38

Death does separate us, at least from each other. The Greek word for "devil" is *diabole,* which means "splitter or separator." That word reminds us that separation by death, to which we're condemned in this life, is an evil. Born for — and called into — community, we suffer deeply when the ties that bind us are broken so utterly. We don't have to pretend it's good. Death is a curse. Or, as a pastor friend of ours put it in his mother's funeral sermon, "Death stinks."

The good news is that it's not the final word. Life is bigger than this life, and the relationships we cherish here are held within the wider circle of love that Paul alludes to in Romans: the "love of God which is in Christ Jesus." The promise of "eternal life" may seem uncomfortingly remote and abstract when we so long for life with our beloved one to continue — mortal, fallible, funny, and warm. And we barely know how to think about eternity; images of the kingdom of heaven range from a family reunion in the sky to a whole new kind of embodiment, free of the time-space limitations we experience in this dimension.

The promise of continuing life offers us hope, but confronts us also with mystery. Is eternity duration in time, or some barely imaginable experience of absolute "nowness"? These are matters for speculation, though the Gospels give us indications, and stories by survivors of near-death experiences — a body of testimony that has grown abundantly and interestingly over the past decades — offer some fairly consistent glimpses of what we may expect: light, welcome, forgiveness, unconditional love, new understanding in a larger context. The ways that many of us have been conditioned to think and theologize about heaven and hell are very likely pale reflections at best of the wider world that awaits us, shaped and suffused by the love of God.

We're here on assignment. We don't fully know or need to know our deepest purposes — only that we are called to live the lives we're given with faith and integrity, to learn to love, and to prepare for a future that is entirely in God's good hands. Letting go of one another as our respective journeys end is a hard part of that assignment. But the day isn't far when we'll go, too. We all finish here and go home. Home, T. S. Eliot writes, is where we start from — a place, Paul assures us, where we are known and where new knowing and more joyous, unimpeded love await us.

In the meantime, separation is real, and weeping does endure for a night — sometimes many nights — when the terms of this life seem hard indeed. In those nights it may be that the best we can do is light one small candle of remembrance that may remind us of God's quiet, abiding presence, the love that surrounds us, and the promise that diminishes this separation to a vanishing point in the larger, longer, truer life we are already living that we call immortality.

*Loving God, be near us in this hard time of loss. Remind us all that our lives are bigger than we know, and that death is not the final word. Give us courage to endure this separation with hope, and give us resolve to live the remainder of the earthly lives we each are given with fidelity and gratitude. We ask in the name of Christ, the one who was truly faithful in life and in death. Amen.*

# WORDS FOR KEEPING WATCH

# A Breath Prayer

*If it is your privilege to keep vigil at the bedside of someone who is dying, you may find that simply breathing with him or her is a way of joining in the slowing rhythms and accompanying the dying person up to the moment of departure. This prayer may be helpful in focusing attention on the breath as a gift that comes and a gift that we release every moment of our lives. Between each sentence or two you might pause for a long, slow breath, remembering that each breath is a gift. Any of the lines may be repeated as often as may be helpful.*

~

Creator God, we receive our breath from you.
We release it back to you.

~

We receive life from your hand.
We offer it back in due time.

~

In life we are yours.
In death we are yours.

~

In sorrow and blessing we began.
As sorrow and blessing we accept this ending.

~

We trust that this ending is a beginning.
We pray for a safe journey as this great door opens.

~

You give and you take away.
All things are yours.

~

Our times are in your hands.
Our lives are in your keeping.

~

Great heart of God, hold us.
Strong arms of God, encircle us.

Holy One who made us, remake us.
Jesus who came for us, come to us.
Spirit who sustains us, see us through.

## One-Line Prayers

*These prayers, too, are "breath prayers" that may serve to sustain a sense of God's presence when words are helpful primarily as ways of entering those silences where the Spirit prays with "sighs too deep for words."*

~

God, our times are in your hands.

~

Thy will be done.

~

Robed in light you come, and are with us in the darkness.

~

Love, bid him/her welcome.

~

I mourn today with those who mourn.
Bless us in our sorrow.

~

All that I am, all that I have comes from you and returns.

# Vigil Affirmations

*Affirmations are short reminders of truth that we may cling to for comfort and assurance in the hardest of times. In a way similar to centering prayer or to "breath prayers," short affirmations may provide a place of return throughout the day. Whenever fear arises, or unease, or distraction, they may bring one's awareness back to the loving presence of God and the faithful witness of the Holy Spirit.*

~

In the hour of death, God watches us.

~

In the hour of death, angels surround us.

~

In the hour of death, saints pray for us.

~

In the hour of death, the Spirit prepares us.

~

In the hour of death, angels minister to us.

~

In the hour of death, Christ meets us.

~

In the hour of death, grace does not fail us.

~

In the hour of death, healing happens.

~

In the hour of death, mystery humbles us.

~

In the hour of death, faith upholds us.

## The Seventh Week: A Vigil

*Poetry often comes in hard times. It leaves its own unique record of pain, loss, and lament. This poem was written at the bedside of a beloved one in the last days before her death. Family took turns at that post. Some came together and talked. Some asked for time alone with her. Some busied themselves with small, practical comforts: moistening her lips, shifting her head on the pillow, adjusting a blanket. A poem is no more or less than another act of attention — a prayer of its own kind, into which may be folded the bitterness, the dread, the hope, the love, the sense of mystery that are all part of keeping vigil.*

~

This week birds in the Gulf were dying.
Their feathers too heavy to lift, they sank
in the ruined watery home whose blue
had upheld them, shining, between earth and sky.

All week she lay with swollen limbs,
language melting on her tongue, eyes
opening and closing again to the faces of those
who came to bid her a safe journey home.

Her slow going made room for song
while her stubborn heart clung to its rhythm,
and breath came with a note like the night wind,
deeper than the voice we knew, and serene.

Something soft opened in the midst of our dread.
She rested, relieved, in her own consent to the going.
Once, awakening, she raised both arms, swayed a little,
and said, so softly we could hardly hear, "Last dance."

An organ failed, and then another. Her blood
grew thin and her strong limbs stilled.
She listened to our refrain — that she was safe,
that she was loved — and to what we could not hear.

Between her sighs we listened, too, into the quiet
of afternoon. On a highway nearby a driver
died. A bomb fell on an Afghan village.
No death modifies any other. Even the most

foreseen shocks us into radical humility.
We do not know. We cannot judge.
We accept, or do not accept, the bitter blessing
of the final hour, its clarity, its violence, its grace.

# A Litany for the Living

*Litany is an ancient liturgical form that, by means of repetition, sustains focus on particular needs, promises, truths, and hopes. Over the centuries, litanies have been written for significant occasions in the liturgical year, and also for use as personal prayers. This one reminds, reassures, and requests as it moves through the felt experience of preparing for imminent loss.*

~

Beloved Creator, you made us for yourself.
Our hearts are restless until they rest in you.
Our minds are restless until they find peace in you.

In you we take our daily rest.
In you we take our final rest.

As we release our beloved one into that final rest,
we ask that you help us do so

without bitterness,
without resentment,
without clinging to the past,
without fear of the future,
without obsessive regret,
without the rage that poisons mourning.

Open our hearts to the blessing
that comes to those who mourn.

Strengthen our confidence
that your promise of eternal life is already fulfilled,
that our earthly journeys, long or short, serve your good
     purposes,
that our times are in your hands.

We lift up in gratitude the life, now completed, of our
     beloved brother/sister.
Let his/her death increase our trust.
Let it increase our hope of heaven.
Let it increase our understanding
   that in your great heart
   and in your strong embrace,
   we find our final home;
   that your love is broader
   than the measures of the mind;
   that life is a gift,
   that death is a release,
   and that in life and in death we are wholly yours.

Fill our hearts with gratitude for the life now ended,
for every good gift he/she brought into our lives,
for every teaching that came through him/her,
for the way he/she served as an agent of grace.

Bless us as we live beyond this loss.
Send us companions with whom we can weep.
Encircle us with your light in our moments of darkness.

Guide us as we continue the lives you have given us to live.
And teach us in all things to give you thanks.

In your gentle presence and in your holy name we pray.
Amen.

# *Permissions*

The author and publisher gratefully acknowledge permission to quote the following material:

In the meditation "Things Take Time": Excerpt from "Her Stroke," reprinted from the book of poems *As When, In Season* by Jim Schley (Marick Press, 2008). All rights reserved. Used with permission of the author.

In the meditation "Untimely, Unseemly": Excerpt from Denise Levertov, "Death Psalm: O Lord of Mysteries," from *Life in the Forest*, copyright © 1978 by Denise Levertov. Reprinted by permission of New Directions Publishing Corp.

In the meditation "Consent and Consolation": Excerpts from Jane Kenyon, "Let Evening Come," from *Collected Poems*. Copyright © 2005 by The Estate of Jane Kenyon. Reprinted with permission of The Permissions Company, Inc., on behalf of Graywolf Press, Minneapolis, Minnesota, www.graywolfpress.org.

In the meditation "Like a Leaf": Excerpt from Wendell Berry, "Prayers and Sayings of the Mad Farmer," from *Farming: A Handbook*. Copyright © 2011 by Wendell Berry. Reprinted by permission of Counterpoint.